Through the Doors of Perception to Heaven via the

Rose Way Meditation

Ascend the sacred chakra stairwell,
develop psychic abilities, spiritual consciousness,
intuition, energy channeling and healing

Dana Williams

Attunement Press

copyright©2013 Dana Williams
Attunement Press
ISBN: 978-0-9795995-6-9
All Rights Reserved

Disclaimer: The entire contents of this book are based on the author's personal experience, unless otherwise noted. The publisher, the author and distributers present this material for educational purposes only. In no way does this book attempt to diagnose or treat any medical or psychological condition, nor to prevent, treat, mitigate or cure such conditions. If you suffer from any medical or psychological condition, consult a licensed physician and ask whether the the practices contained within this book could interfere with your existing care, and if they are safe and harmless for you, before you begin to use them.

"If the doors of perception *were cleansed every thing would appear to man as it is, Infinite. For man has closed himself up, till he sees all things thro' narrow chinks of his cavern."*
—William Blake

Table of Contents

Introduction by Dr. Todd Michael ... 9

Note from the Author ... 12

Preface ... 15

CHAPTER ONE - Introducing the *Rose Way* Meditation ... 19

Impressions and Recollections ... 19

Learning the Technique ... 21

CHAPTER TWO - An Overview of the Basics ... 23

Invocation: Asking ... 23

Visualization with God's White Light ... 24

For Those Who Cannot Visualize ... 25

Sensing the Qualities of the Light ... 25

Light Qualities Exercise ... 26

Self-Control for Meditation ... 29

The Motion of Light ... 29

Spiraling Energy Exercise ... 30

CHAPTER THREE - Preparing for the *Rose Way* Meditation ... 31

Grounding, the *Rose Way* ... 31

Daily Practice of Charging, Grounding and Protection ... 32

Exercise: Energetic Charging through the Feet ... 33

More Tips for Grounding ... 35

Buddhist Grounding Meditations ... 36

CHAPTER FOUR - The *Rose Way* Up and Down the Chakras ... 37

Joe's Horizontal View of the Chakras ... 37

Joe's Horizontal View of the Chakras ... 37

The Release of Dark and Stagnant Conditions ... 37

Final Preparatory Steps for the *Rose Way* Meditation ... 39

Chakra Opening Preparation ... 39

Chakra Opening and Expansion ... 40

Chakra Opening ... 40

Closing Down ... 42

Chakra Closing and Grounding ... 42

Chakra Closing ... 43

CHAPTER FIVE - The Level of the Rose ... 45

The Rose as a Symbol and Experience of Self ... 45

Ascending to the Level of the Rose ... 46

CHAPTER SIX - The Levels of Heaven, the Evolution of Souls ... 51

Joe's Description of the Four Higher Levels ... 51

Ascending to the Higher Levels ... 52

Directions to the Levels ... 53

Michael Newton's Description of Soul Levels ... 53

The "White Level" ... 56

Meditation on the White Level ... 56

Inviting Your Guides ... 56

CHAPTER SEVEN - Exercise to Completely Close the Chakras ... 59

Closing the Chakras ... 60

Spacing the Full Meditation ... 63

CHAPTER EIGHT - Practicing the Higher Senses ... 65

Laws for Communication with the "Other Side" ... 65

About Guides ... 68

Interacting with our Guides ... 69

Rest and Restoration ... 71

Communication with your Guides ... 73

Receiving Messages in Daily Life ... 75

Remote Viewing ... 77

Respectful Viewing ... 79

Getting Visuals—A Reminder ... 81

Receiving a Personalized Meditation Form ... 82

Contact with the Deceased ... 83

Birth Announcements ... 84

Past Lives ... 84

Seeing the Future ... 86

Meeting our Demons ... 87

Healing ... 88

Responding to a Cold or Flu ... 88

White Light Clearing ... 89

Stopping a Sore Throat:
Focusing God's Healing Energy through Your Hands ... 89

Circling Energy for Multiple Healing Applications ...91

CHAPTER NINE - *Rose Way* Meditation ... 92

Phase One – Invocation ... 92

Phase Two – Charging ... 92

Phase Three - Chakra Opening ... 93

Phase Four - Ascending to the Level of the Rose ... 94

Phase Five - Ascending to the White Level ... 95

Phase Six - Individual Meditation ... 95

Phase Seven - Psychic Exercises ... 95

Phase Eight - Descending to the Rose ... 96

Phase Nine - Chakra Closing ... 97

CHAPTER TEN - Who was Joe Koperski? ... 100

An Interview with David St. Clair ... 101

Three Personal Teachings ... 105

Evening Classes ... 106

Saturday Morning Classes ... 107

Joe's Energy Healing ... 108

Closing Words ... 109

APPENDIX ... 111

Recommended Reading ... 111

Introduction

As a retired trauma and emergency physician, and the author of *The Evolution Angel* and *The Twelve Conditions of a Miracle*--winner of the *Nebula Award* in New York, for "Best Spiritual Book of the Year 2005"— it is my distinct honor and pleasure to introduce to you this fascinating and wholly original book by Dana Williams, called *Through the Doors of Perception to Heaven, via the Rose Way Meditation*.

I have written many books on spiritual and metaphysical subjects, and have taught and spoken extensively about yoga, meditation, energy healing, and other related subjects at venues like the Art Bell Show, Edgar Cayce's A.R.E. in Virginia, and many others. Through my experience, I have become well-acquainted with the spectrum of books and teachings that are available to people seeking to improve themselves, to increase their knowledge about meditation, raise their conscious awareness, and otherwise maximize their potential as human beings. Yet, in all my travels and meetings with scores of teachers, mentors, gurus, and great monks, I have never encountered a meditation like the *Rose Way*. It is completely non-derivative, new, and unique. It offers a distinct way of expanding one's awareness that cannot be achieved through other means, yet is completely compatible with and complimentary to other disciplines.

Those who have practiced meditation for many years— including things like TM or Transcendental Meditation, Zen and

Buddhist meditations, various types of Judeo-Christian meditation, those related to the venerable traditions of yoga, and other more esoteric varieties, will find the new and challenging sequence of the *Rose Way* to be a refreshingly more complex and astonishingly effective adjunct to their practices.

Practitioners of the *Rose Way* will often report that they are "breaking out of their plateaus" and reaching new unrealized heights of consciousness. Many will find themselves unexpectedly accessing or enhancing their true potentials for such abilities as remote viewing, communication with spirit guides and departed souls across the veil, achieving more power and control of their healing energies, and experiencing an overall increase in *intuition*. These abilities can be extremely valuable for healers and psychics, particularly when dealing with difficult physical disorders and psycho-emotional problems.

Most people would agree that we do not yet completely understand the human mind-body complex—the mechanisms through which the incredible human organism can know, see, heal, and create positive circumstances for our loved ones and ourselves. In fact, if truth be told, in another one or two hundred years we will look back at what we now "know" as almost childlike in its naiveté. Both science and spirituality are advancing at a formidable, increasingly exponential rate, and it is through higher forms of meditation such as the *Rose Way* that some of our best advances will be realized.

Be prepared: Through the practices formulated in this book, to have your understandings challenged and your perceptions rearranged. Be prepared, quite literally, to step through what William Blake, and subsequently the visionary Aldous Huxley called, the "doors of perception," which lead to the realm of light, to oneness, to home...to Heaven. It could be said by those that study it, that the *Rose Way* meditation could be the most expanding and transformative meditation that has yet been devised. Without a doubt, Spirit has given this great door of love and light to us now, as a significant tool in our continuing exploration of consciousness.

Many blessings to you and yours as you make your way to the Light.

—Dr. Todd Michael, June, 2013

Note from the Author

I have wanted to share this unique and powerful meditation with the wider public for a long time, but have hesitated. After all, not I, but my deceased teacher, Joe Koperski, received this meditation from his own ascended master teacher, Lu Sen, back in the 1960s.

About a year ago, I was introduced to the writing of clinical psychologist and hypnotherapist, Dr. Michael Newton Ph.D. With fascination, I read through his book *Journey of Souls: Case Studies of Life between Lives*, and then its sequel, *Destiny of Souls: New Case Studies of Life Between Lives*. The authority of Newton's work took me by surprise. With each page, I learned something new. Yet, in its entirety, Dr. Newton's information also encompassed and embraced everything I had previously learned or understood about the nature of the soul's evolution. For me, reading his work was a paradigm shift.

One day, as I thought about Newton's work, I realized that the unique meditation form I had learned from Joe Koperski decades ago aligns with and corroborates Newton's case studies. As I contemplated the resonance between Dr. Newton's work and Joe's teaching, I realized that Joe's meditation could possibly be highly relevant for today's seeker. I began to form a resolve to write up Joe's meditation, and as I did so, I felt my teacher's presence and his smile of encouragement near me.

Still, there were those inevitable moments that all authors experience, when I felt unsure of myself again. Perhaps I was taking on too much? Was it really my place to teach others this powerful meditation? Were Joe's revelations really mine to tell?

On one such day of uncertainty and doubt, I practiced the *Rose Way* meditation, and remained in a Zen-like attitude of relaxed, mindful focus. All of a sudden, I heard the words spoken, "She should consult...."

Feeling like a child, eaves-dropping on the conversation of one's elders, I perked my inner ears and listened. I heard a name. I heard it spoken slowly, over-articulated, as if to make sure that I really "got it": "T-o-d-d M-i-c-h-a-e-l."

Surprised and energized, I hurried to my laptop and began to type. In no time at all, I'd found Dr. Michael's website, and ordered his books.

To have been told exactly whom I should consult—concerning the book I was writing—was initially quite a shock. However, I had received this information while performing Joe's meditation. I had opened my chakras and ascended to the "White Level," where such exchanges with spiritual guides are much more accessible. I needed to trust myself, to trust my inner teachers, and to understand that in receiving this name, my deeper concern—about whether or not I should truly write this book—had been answered. Source had directed me to a "consultant;" Source wanted me to write this book!

After reading my manuscript, Dr. Michael, himself a great and natural intuitive, began to practice the *Rose Way* meditation. He soon related to me that he felt a clear, inner connection to my teacher, Joe Koperski, and to Lu Sen as well.

Dr. Michael addressed my concerns and answered my writing and publishing questions; and his boundless enthusiasm for the *Rose Way* energized me to stay focused and write the book. I am quite sure that Dr. Michael's advice and influence enabled Joe's teaching and his vibrational quality to be fully expressed and embodied within these pages. Thank you Dr. Michael! "Someone" surely knew what they were doing when they recommended you to me!

This book would not have been possible without the help of one other extraordinary person—my daughter. She took time off from her busy college schedule to sit with me hour after hour, week after week, to read through many drafts of this book, and to help me craft a clear and easy-to-understand presentation. Thank you, my dear!

Preface

This book presents *The Rose Way Meditation*, or *Rose Way*, for short. I had the honor to study this meditation from 1973–1975 with Joe Koperski, a healer, psychic, and meditation teacher in Los Angeles. Joe, in turn, received this meditation from the wise and loving spirit of Lu Sen, an ascended master teacher whose last incarnation here on Earth was in 6th century China.

While the *Rose Way* is particularly well-suited for those with a background in metaphysics or other forms of meditation, it can also be quite useful and accessible to those who are just learning to meditate.

The *Rose Way* directs practitioners to expand their chakras horizontally, like platforms or rungs on a ladder. While this might sound unusual, the process will soon become clear and even second nature as you follow the simple instructions in this book.

Upon the levels of *horizontal* chakra expansion, the practitioner then ascends *vertically* up the chakra ladder, rising above the head, to the eighth chakra that Joe called our "Spiritual Rose." From here, it is possible for those who are ready to ascend to higher levels still. Joe explained that when we ascend the *Rose Way*, we pass through the astral level and on to the spiritual realm, where human consciousness is greatly expanded. For many practitioners, spiritual awareness and psychic phenomena then become naturally and effortlessly accessible.

One of the most exciting prospects regarding the *Rose Way* is that it can be adapted for use in diverse fields. In 2009, I published two books that describe applications based on the

Rose Way. The first, *Math by Grace,* is geared to the education of primary school children. With this method, I was able to successfully help three of my own children, whose learning problems included hyperactivity and Asperger's Syndrome, to memorize their basic math. Immediately after practicing the *Math by Grace* visualization, my children grew so confident in their math skills that they went from the lower thirds to the tops of their classes.

This experience reinforced my confidence in the *Rose Way*'s ability to help children, and adults as well, through a kind of energetic re-programming of the body-mind, so that learners can more easily absorb, understand and recall all kinds of information—even in areas where they previously may have been struggling. I encourage parents, therapists, healers, and educational specialists everywhere to look into this new method of working with the human mind.

My second book, *The Lord's Prayer, The Seven Chakras, The Twelve Life Paths,* describes a powerful, healing and grounding prayer-meditation. It too, derives its strong and immediate effects from its foundation on the *Rose Way* meditation.

In spiritual literature, there are many terms and metaphors that derive from the same universal experiences and concepts. I want to note at the outset, that in this book I will use spiritual language as Joe Koperski consistently used it, including free use of traditional terms such as "God" rather than Source, Spirit, Higher Self, or other more contemporary terms and expressions. The eighth chakra will be referred to as the *Rose*. Because Joe used the terms "God's Energy," "White Light," and "White Healing Energy," I will follow suit. He also spoke of "energy levels" rather than of "densities" or "dimensions," and I will do the same.

Of course, as you are reading this book, you may long ago have transcended any concern about terminology: many names exist for the same Great Being and for the Heavens, and all are worthy of the highest respect.

By activating the aura's capacity to expand, to open, and to evolve, Joe Koperski offers us a method to easily access higher energy states and their concurrent psychic abilities. The exercises that Joe created for psychic development were based on a system that he had channeled called "Chaldean Astrology and Numerology." A book on this may one day be available, but for now I will offer a set of exercises that are based on my own psychic experiences with Joe's meditation. These are sure to compliment any exercises that you might otherwise be practicing.

Joe's greater objective, however, and his wish for his students, and for all spiritual seekers, was that we grow in spiritual awareness while becoming knowledgeable and empowered human beings, each traveling on their own individual path.

Here are some of the ways in which the *Rose Way* may be of value to you:

o It may give quick access to deep experiences of spirituality.

o It may intensify and compliment other styles of meditation.

o It may enhance psychic abilities, such as telepathy, clairvoyance, and clairaudience.

o It may help those who work intuitively with symbol-sets such as astrology, I Ching or the tarot.

o It may enhance and intensify healing modalities based on energy work.

o It may help contact to spiritual guides become increasingly conscious and accessible.

o The *Rose Way* may increase awareness of personal life contracts and choices, leading naturally to greater joy, confidence and energy.

—Dana Williams   2013

CHAPTER ONE -

Introducing the *Rose Way* Meditation

Impressions and Recollections

Though I want to quickly proceed to the heart of the matter—the *Rose Way* and how to practice it—I would be remiss if I did not first say a few words about my teacher. To begin, I will briefly share my memories of the first time that I met Joe Koperski, and in the last chapter I will write more about my beloved teacher and his classes.

Arriving at Joe's house, that first time in September, 1972, I felt a bit tremulous. I was seventeen years of age and had just recently begun practicing yoga and meditation on my own. When a teacher at my high school told me about Joe's class, I could hardly believe my ears. "An actual class where you can learn how to meditate?"

It must be appreciated that classes on yoga and meditation were not at all common back then, nor did the Internet exist where a teacher could advertise themselves with a website. Tips were shared solely by word of mouth, and to receive such information seemed a tremendous stroke of good fortune.

Joe's house was located on a busy street in what was then a struggling part of town. A tiny flowerbed added a touch of green to the front of the house, and an ice cream franchise close by kept its lights burning and its doors open until midnight. There was nothing particularly striking or unusual to be seen—at least on the physical plane.

I knocked, and an older woman welcomed me. I followed her through the small foyer in which a tiny table displayed a basket for donations, next to a few candles and incense for sale.

In a largish, impersonal room, about twenty people sat on folding chairs that were arranged in concentric rows. I found an empty chair, squeezed myself onto it, and waited. The air was heavy with incense, and a radio played classical music softly in the background.

Sitting there with my eyes closed, and surrounded by strangers, I became aware of the traffic noise on the busy street outside. Then I noticed the rattling of all the windowpanes, as heavier vehicles passed by. *How can anyone concentrate with all this racket?* I thought to myself. But as the minutes went by, I grew surprisingly calm.

Then the lights and the radio were switched off, and in the center of the room, a man began to speak—warmly, reassuringly, and at a comfortable pace about God, Light, and Self Control. What he said was utterly new to me, yet it was easy to follow the instructions as he guided us into meditation.

Soon, I was no longer conscious of the sound of the tires on the street, or of the glass shaking in the window frames. I no longer smelled the incense. A new space opened up. How can I describe it? It was comfortable and cozy, like a wolf's den, a place buried deep within myself, *here*, in the center of me.

I thought, astonished, "I have found a completely new part of myself." With fascination, I continued to follow his words. The meditation deepened. The inner space widened, gained depth and dimension.

I was hooked. This feeling—that I believe you too will find if you follow along and practice this meditation—was as though meeting myself for the first time. Many spiritual teachers have called this experience a "realization of Self," or one of "coming home." For me, at age seventeen, it was accompanied by an acute sense of surprise: that within myself I could discover such unknown terrain!

Over the next two years, I would attend Joe's classes as often as possible. I became one of his most ardent students, as well as his youngest by far. In spite of the fact that I saw him three to four times a week, however, he remained somewhat of an enigma. At times, I couldn't even recall exactly what he looked like except in the most generalized terms: that his features were both soft and rugged, his smiling eyes dark, and his eyebrows shaggy. Some people are like that—their features so subtle that you can hardly take them in.

What I do remember, and vividly, is his spirit, his kindness. Most importantly, however, I remember his teachings. I'll share more about my teacher, Joe Koperski, in Chapter Ten, but for now, dear reader, we will proceed directly to the meditation itself.

Learning the technique

In the following chapters, we will carefully walk through each part of the *Rose Way* meditation technique. This information will be presented in a workbook format, which will enable you to stop, practice, and learn each component at your own pace.

I strongly recommend that you keep a journal to note your experiences and impressions as you learn each step. (I shall be publishing a "Rose Way Journal" for those who appreciate extra guidance in the journaling process—look for it online.) Treat this journal with special regard, for it will serve you well and become a friend to you as you make your way along the journey.

Once you have understood and practiced the entire meditation, you will find that it is not at all difficult to do from memory. At the outset, however, it may seem a bit challenging. That's normal and to be expected.

The complete meditation form, with all the sections fitted together, can be found in Chapter Nine. By the time you have arrived at Chapter Nine, you will doubtless have mastered the steps and will easily know them by heart. Should you like to make yourself a recording of the meditation, you can read the instructions onto a recording device. Most all computers and cell phones have simple recorders built right into them. Also, a low cost digital recorder can be purchased at any average discount store or online. In addition, an audiobook is in the planning on which I will read several variations of this meditation. Look for it in 2014.

CHAPTER TWO –

An Overview of the Basics

The sections below explain the invocation, visualization, and the contemplation of the "Light." With these practices, you will quickly find a firm footing on the *Rose Way*.

The Invocation: Asking

To speak an invocation is to respectfully request that something based in spiritual energy—such as God's Blessings, Light, Energy, Peace, or Love—be brought into, or made manifest within one's own awareness.

To begin the *Rose Way* meditation, we close our eyes, quietly focus our attention within, and *ask* sincerely that God's Light come to us.

To some, it may seem paradoxical to ask that God's Energy or Light come to us. After all, if one accepts that God exists, wouldn't God be everywhere at all times? Why invoke something that is already here?

The answer is that this respectful "asking" is not done to attract God's attention to us, but rather for *us to become aware of God's presence*. When we invoke God's White Light, we remind our subconscious minds to become aware of and attuned to what is already here.

By focusing on God's Energy, the aura begins to resonate with it and to gravitate and evolve toward it. As we become more attuned to God's White Light, we automatically place our focus in the *here and now*, which is the only "place" we can find and know God.

We could also invoke the Light by saying: "I ask my mind to become aware of, and in tune with, the Light that is always *here*, and the enlightenment that I always *am*." If you are more comfortable with this kind of approach, feel free to use it—I often do. But throughout this book I will use the form that Joe consistently used to phrase his invocations to God.

Visualization with God's White Light

Our invocation is followed by visualizing the White Light. Through our intention to visualize the Light, we develop a greater sensitivity and responsiveness to this endless source of strength, confidence, and universal love.

Initially, we might suspect that we are merely inventing images while visualizing. This is entirely normal. When I first began to study with Joe, I struggled with this issue. Whenever I tried to "see" the Light, I felt as though I was "just imagining it." Eventually, I would come to understand that my imagination could function as a kind of "meeting place" or "interface" between my subjective world and the so-called objective, spiritual realities. The most important step in this process was allowing myself to *trust in and work with* my imagination rather than doubting and second-guessing it. The more I trusted my imagination, the stronger and clearer my visualizations became.

By exercising the part of the brain that forms images, we activate our inner sensory abilities, similar to stretching and strengthening a muscle. The faculty of consciousness that can synthesize images is one of the most highly evolved powers of the mind. And, just like a muscle, the more that it is used, the stronger it gets.

For Those Who Cannot Visualize

Some people, try as they might, cannot visualize well at all. While the ability to visualize is helpful, and it can develop and become stronger with time, visualization is not inherently necessary to the *Rose Way* meditation. There is a kind of "knowing" that can serve you just as well. To access this during the *Rose Way* meditation, practice *knowing* that you are being enveloped in the White Light, *knowing* that the energy is circling and opening your chakras, etc.

For some people, *knowing,* too, is difficult. They need not worry. They may be able to *feel, trust, intuit,* or *believe.*

Whether you choose to visualize, know, trust, intuit or believe, the two sections below will help you experience the Light.

Sensing the Qualities of the Light

Joe ascribed six qualities to the Light: Peace, Love, Harmony, Balance, Self-Control, and Human Understanding. Whenever he invoked the White Energy of God he would speak these qualities aloud, slowly, and pause after each to give us time to resonate with the mental and emotional associations that each word evoked. In this way, Joe encouraged the development of two more mental "muscles" which are essential for deeper meditation: active listening and inner participation.

Interestingly, Joe's qualities do not include words such as excitement, joy, ecstasy, or brilliance. Such energies are prone to flow outwards, to be dispersed, whereas Joe's qualities are quieter and more focused. The energetic qualities invoked by these words will concentrate within the body and aura, where they nourish, build, and maintain our energetic structure.

The Light Qualities Exercise

Begin by sitting or lying quietly. Relax your body and mind, and focus on the positive associations that come to you with respect to each of the qualities: Peace, Love, Harmony, Balance, Self-Control, and Human Understanding. Give yourself time for their resonance, also called attunements, to spread like a vibration throughout your body-mind before proceeding from one quality to the next.

At first, it might seem arduous to enter the "space" that each quality holds for you. With time and practice, however, your mind will naturally embrace the qualities of the Light. You will then experience a quicker deepening of your basic meditation state, as each quality almost instantly spreads through your body-mind.

To begin, try to recall special experiences from your life while contemplating each quality. It can be useful to jot down these key memories and their associated sensations in your meditation journal. These will then be readily available to jog your memory as you repeat the exercise later. For example:

Peace—Recall memories of when you were near the ocean, contemplating a vast snowscape, or lying in a meadow beneath a starry sky, when you felt "taken up" into something greater than yourself, safe and secure in the certain knowing that all is well.

Peace has a transcendent and eternal feeling to it. It is timeless, expansive, both personal and impersonal, and deeply comforting. Find *your* images, your most evocative memories of peace, and stay with them until you feel their essence saturating your body-mind.

Love—Recall memories of warmth and happiness when your heart opened in a powerful and genuine way. Perhaps this was while you were holding a beloved pet, or when deeply bonded and experiencing true intimacy and affection with a special partner, friend, child, or parent.

Love embodies a sense of well-being and good-will toward all. In its essence it is boundless. Love is not a feeling that originates from within the head, or the mind, but rather from your core, your heart. While a specific person or event may trigger the feeling, if it is true love, it transcends that specific person and radiates outwards to encompass everyone and everything in your world. Find *your* images, your own treasured memories of authentic love and stay with them, delving deeply into the associated sensations, until the essence of love saturates your entire body-mind.

Harmony—Recall memories of activities, alone or with others, at play or at work, when everything was joyfully flowing and cooperative; recall experiences when you were effortlessly in "the zone," such as a time when you were practicing an art form, sport, or other activity with special ease, grace, and accuracy.

Harmony imbues the mind with an appreciation of beauty, rapport, congruity, and proportion. "Harvest" the bodily and mental sensations associated with your memories until the feeling of harmony saturates your entire body-mind.

Balance—Recall memories of instances when you could say either yes or no to life's offerings and demands, while staying within moderation. Think of times when you were able to stay level and stable, when you were able to navigate through conflict or meet life's challenges with serenity, equanimity, maturity, and steadiness.

Balance is the ability to maneuver between life's extremes without losing perspective or being pulled into reactive, excessive, or addictive behavior. Stay with your images or memories of your balanced experiences until the deep, quiet self-confidence that comes with that balance saturates your body-mind.

Self-control—Recall and honor times when you have exercised mature restraint, when you did what you knew was right, was healthful, and beneficial for others and yourself.

The quality of Self-Control can also be accessed in memories where you cultivated good habits, successfully committed to keeping up with the demands of daily life, and did what was needed to activate and unfold positive future plans. At times, exercising self-control involves delaying gratification, or calming yourself when you become upset.

Make note of these successful incidences of self-control in your meditation journal. The same feelings of self-control will help you stay focused when you are meditating.

Human Understanding—Human Understanding is recognizing our collective striving to become better human beings with greater humility, gratitude, and a realistic point of view, and our desire to grow beyond arrogance, bias, bitterness, gullibility and naïve idealism.

Human understanding is genuinely compassionate, because we understand from the heart that all humans are capable of wonderful things, but also that we are frail and flawed. When you practice human understanding you are not taken in by the guile of others, or sidetracked by your own self-seeking pride. You understand the spectrum of human behavior, while striving to be the best that you can be.

To access memories and sensations that will help you experience this quality of the Light, recall times when you were able to make wise decisions based on your human experience. Sense that through our human understanding and our attunement to God's Light, humanity is capable of transformation.

Self-Control for Meditation

Joe ascribed a special meaning to "self-control" as it pertains specifically to the process of meditation. He said that it is through self-control that we concentrate on pure, positive states. Through self-control, we devote this time to our attunement with God, and we banish all worries and concerns. It is with the power of self-control that we expand the chakras and ascend through them to the spheres, and it is with self-control that we later close down the chakras. Joe also said that Lu Sen had given us the image of the *Rose* to aid our self-control within the opening process.

The Motion of Light

Joe asked us to visualize the Light as moving *in a circular and spiraling motion*. Visualizing this motion, he said, aids in charging the chakras, so that we can access higher energy levels for our meditation, healing and psychic work.

He drew many parallels to nature in this regard, pointing out where circular and spiral patterns are found in abundance, from the microscopic and subatomic levels to the largest astronomical of patterns—from the tiny double helix of an exquisite DNA molecule, to the fractal unfolding of the snail's shell, to the swirling, helical patterns of weather systems, and on to the unfurling of entire galaxies.

Spiraling Energy Exercise:

o You can do this exercise either sitting or lying down.

o First, inhale and exhale deeply three times.

o Then, say mentally, or out loud: "I ask that God's White Light enter this room in a circular motion, and rise from the floor to the ceiling."

Feel the reality of the energy as it spirals upwards from the floor in small and large vortices—like a gentle, whirling wind. It spirals up to the ceiling, filling the room with gracious clouds that catch rays of sunlight in their whiteness. Feel the energy as it fills all the spaces in the room—beneath the furniture, in all the corners, and as it penetrates the walls and windows. Allow, and trust the powers of your imagination to guide you.

o Now say, "I ask that God's White Light encircle my body." Visualize the Light enveloping and encircling your body, as in a sheath of one or two inches. Then visualize the Light enveloping and encircling your body at about six inches. Then visualize it at twelve inches, and finally at two feet.

o After concentrating the White Light around your body in this manner, inhale and exhale deeply three times. Express your gratitude to God for this gift of awareness and attunement.

o Open your eyes and check in with yourself. Compare how you feel now to when you began the exercise, and note your observations in your meditation journal.

CHAPTER THREE –

Preparing for the *Rose Way* Meditation

Before practicing the full *Rose Way* meditation, it is important to repeat the following exercises until they feel natural and come easily:

Grounding,

the daily charging exercise,

chakra opening,

chakra closing.

Grounding, the Rose Way

Joe taught that there are two main pathways to invite God's Energy into the body: through the feet, and through the top of the head. He explained that when God's Energy enters through the feet, it carries a grounding, vitalizing, earthy quality. When it enters through the top of the head, it carries a spiritual, heavenly, opening quality.

Joe advised us to charge ourselves *through the feet* at least once a day. To the new practitioner, grounding may not sound particularly important, and might easily be neglected. It *is* important, however.

When spiritual seekers begin to raise their frequencies and to charge their psychic centers, it is possible that they could suffer from psychic burnout or become energetically imbalanced. This can be prevented through the daily practice of grounding—

bringing in downward flowing energies that anchor one's consciousness securely within the body.

Joe explained that if we do not ground properly, and our centers remain open, we might find ourselves picking up on psychic signals much like an antennae or wireless router. This might feel as though our heads are abuzz with entities that want us to listen to their messages. If we listen to these voices more closely, however, we usually discover that they contain nothing that is really important, and that they are more akin to static than to "messages." This can be controlled and "turned off" through grounding.

Much has been written about grounding and its importance. In her book *Eastern Body, Western Mind*, Anodea Judith writes, "Being grounded gives us a source of strength through connection to our body and environment. Physically this happens through the legs and feet..."

At the end of the exercise described below, we return with the energy back into the feet, and then down into the earth. If done with proper concentration, your energy bodies will now be locked solidly into your physical body, just as should be.

The Daily Practice of Charging, Grounding and Protection

Charging the physical and energy bodies with God's White Energy is an essential preparation for the opening of the chakras. Practice the exercise below *every day*. Within a few weeks, you'll be able to complete it in a matter of seconds, any place and time.

Exercise: Energetic Charging through the Feet

For this exercise, you can be lying, sitting, or standing.

o Close your eyes and breathe deeply in and out, three times.

o Ask silently or out loud that God's White Energy fill the room from the floor to the ceiling in a circular motion.

o As you visualize the Light, ask that God's Light impart its qualities of Peace, Love, Harmony, Balance, Self-Control, and Human Understanding. Feel yourself become attuned to the Light.

o Ask that God's Energy come to you as two globes of White Light that you see and sense below the soles of your feet.

o Invite God's White Energy to enter your body through your feet in a circular motion, and ask it to charge each cell of your body. Mentally follow the Energy as the two globes of Light enter your feet and ascend up your calves to your knees, and through your thighs to your hips.

o Repeat these words to yourself: "God's Light imparts its qualities of Peace, Love, Harmony, Balance, Self-Control, and Human Understanding within me."

o Mentally follow the Light as it ascends up through your torso to your shoulders, then down through your arms, through your elbows and into your hands, and out through your fingers.

o The Energy concentrates momentarily as a globe in the palm of each hand, and then returns through your fingers into your hands and arms as it ascends to your shoulders.

o The Light circles up through your neck into your head, and throughout your skull to the top of your head.

o God's Light imparts Peace, Love, Harmony, Balance, Self-Control, and Human Understanding.

o Now ask that you receive a protective shield in the form of a crystal helmet that covers the top of your head. This step is called "capping the energy system."

o Imagine a transparent and luminescent fabric, like a large white silken sheet or scarf, wrapping softly around your physical body.

o Mentally circle down through your body and return with the Light into your feet, and out through your feet into the earth. Imagine the Light returning deep into the Earth, even to its very center.

o Now visualize the luminescent cloth wrapping about your feet.

o Feel grounded in your body, and connected to the earth.

o Know that your body and mind are recharged with pure, positive energy.

o Conclude the exercise by speaking a few personal words of gratitude.

The wrapping visualization at the end of the exercise insures that your energy body stays well connected to your physical body. It also functions as a protective shield and helps you maintain healthy boundaries. You are now better protected from people who consciously or unconsciously might wish to feed upon and deplete your energy. Do not talk much about your new spiritual practice: talking about it disperses the energies. Keep your new energy close to you like a treasured secret. Stay safe, centered, and grounded.

More Tips for Grounding

Staying grounded is an art. Awareness of lifestyle choices and their influences on grounding can be helpful, and it will become increasingly important for you to be discerning and conscious in your choices of the energies you allow to enter your system. This includes the music you select, the books you read, the foods you choose to eat, and the interpersonal relationships you cultivate.

You cannot control everything, and need not try to. Just be reasonably conscious of these influences, and what you allow to access and enter your sensory mechanisms and your body-mind. Here are a few suggestions to help with grounding:

o Eat a whole-foods diet, and eat small meals frequently, every 2-3 hours, to keep your blood sugar steady.

o For some people, eating organic and humanely produced meat helps with grounding.

o Avoid chemical additives and so-called "excitotoxins" in food such as MSG. Avoid GMOs as much as possible. Limit your intake of caffeine to a level that is good for you. Generally speaking, the less caffeine you can get by with, the better. Try a reduction, or even elimination process to see if this helps.

o Maintain a healthy sleeping schedule.

o Spend less time in front of the many screens that now occupy our lives.

o Exercise—biking, walking, yoga, working your muscles (and if you are disabled, *imagining* that you are working your muscles). Being in touch with our body through movement helps us be grounded.

o Cultivate a regular practice of deep relaxation.

If all of the above is still insufficient, look into heavy metal detoxification (per Andy Cutler's protocol) and consider the possible influence of electromagnetic fields around your bedroom and home, and from sources such as smart phones and smart meters. If you continue to experience significant grounding difficulties, it is probably a good idea to stop meditating until you resolve these issues and establish a solid and firmly grounded balance. Obtain consultation from a healthcare provider—such as a Naturopath, environmental doctor or a qualified therapist—if you are experiencing any significant health problems.

Buddhist Grounding Meditations

To assist with grounding, the Buddhist traditions of meditating at the abdominal center, called the "Hara" or "Dan Tien," can be most helpful. This practice is performed during simple sitting meditation. The meditative focus, when directed upon the lower abdomen, leads spontaneously to deeper union with the physical body and to better grounding.

You might prefer to practice T'ai Chi or Chi Gong, two gentle martial arts techniques that are designed to build up the body's grounding energies and to focus them in one's "center." Should you be unable to devote time to develop these arts, even the practice of their warm-up exercise routines will lead to good results.

Many excellent instructional videos can be found online that show and teach these practices.

CHAPTER FOUR -

The *Rose Way* Up and Down the Chakras

Joe's Horizontal View of the Chakras

Joe Koperski presented us with a new element of chakra dynamics: he described the chakras as horizontal levels that can be sensed in one's energy system like rungs on a ladder. Each chakra core is surrounded by three bands of energy that Joe described as "positive," "negative," and "neutral." When we charge these bands in the chakra opening exercise, the platforms are expanded and can easily be perceived. These platforms then become a foundation upon which the practitioner ascends into the full *Rose Way* meditation. While this may sound unusual and complex, with practice it will soon become accessible and even second nature.

Joe emphasized that in the *Rose Way* meditation, it is not important to work with different colors for the individual chakras, as is commonly done in other forms of chakra healing. He elucidated that because White Light contains all colors within it, if specific colors are needed by a chakra, they are automatically extracted from the Light and used in the balancing of that chakra.

The Release of Dark and Stagnant Conditions

The concept that individuals might be weighted down by a kind of energetic burden (karma, sin, pain-body, ego attachment) is very ancient, as is also the idea that certain practices or adept spiritual teachers can remove that burden from us.

In Hinduism, it is thought that our personal "karma" holds us in bondage. Karmic debt, which is roughly analogous to "sin," can be removed from the devoted disciple in some cases by a guru who "burns" it off through meditation, or who endures physical suffering in the stead of the disciple. For instance, the famed guru Yogananda was seen to age severely and to temporarily need a wheelchair after giving healing services[i]. In this way, the guru shortens and straightens the devotee's path to enlightenment.

In Christianity, it is said that both original and personal "sins" hold us in bondage. Seemingly, there is nothing we ourselves can do to remove this debt. Christian doctrine teaches that through an act of sacrificial suffering, however, Christ has taken this debt upon himself so that the devoted Christian can experience forgiveness, renewal, and rebirth.

In Buddhism, "compassion meditation" is seen as a way to release our energy burdens. In this practice, the Buddhist visualizes inhaling the pain of suffering—both their own pain and the pain of other's—into their heart chakra, where it is cleansed and brought back to a state of pure positivity.

I have found that as the chakras are opened through the *Rose Way* meditation, mental, emotional and physical conditions are naturally saturated with higher energy and are released or transformed. During this process, and while we are on the higher levels, our guides will lend insights, colors, and articles of healing modalities, even imagery and insights from past lives as needed—always in accordance with our abilities to process these energies and information.

Final Preparatory Steps for the Rose Way Meditation

The following three exercises develop the beginning and closing phases of the Rose Way meditation. They should be fully understood, practiced, and come easily before you proceed to the full meditation form.

Chakra Opening Preparation

o Begin by invoking God's Light with its six qualities.

o Visualize it circling around your body and throughout the room in which you sit.

o Now say, "May God's Energy enter my body through the crown of my head."

o Visualize the white energy concentrated above your head, and then sense the Light circling down into your head.

o Ask that the Light come to you with its qualities of Peace, Love, Harmony, Balance, Self-Control, and Human Understanding.

o The Light continues to fill your body, always moving in a circular motion, down through your head and neck to your shoulders, down the arms, into your hands and out through the fingers.

o Shake the hands three times to complete the flow of energy through the fingers and to release any stagnant energy.

o The Light returns up the arms to the shoulders, then circles down through your torso and spine to the hips.

o You may have become aware of tension or energy blocks within or around your physical body. Ask that the Light release these conditions. Breathe deeply, and see the energy block dispersing as the area fills with light.

o From your hips, spiral with the Light down into your feet, then out through your feet and into the ground.

o Pause and feel the open flow of current into the ground. Then return with the Light into your feet, up your legs and into your hips.

o Here at the base of the spine, you are at the level of the first chakra, and ready to commence chakra opening.

Chakra Opening and Expansion

As previously explained, Joe viewed the seven main chakras as horizontal platforms or levels. He explained that each chakra has a core that is in alignment with the spine, surrounded by three concentric bands that are charged: negative, positive, and neutral.

When you first begin this exercise, the individual bands of the chakra may feel as though they are about one inch across. With repeated charging and practice, you will feel the bands thicken and expand. In a few months time, they may grow several inches deeper, and the platforms of the open and expanded chakras may extend well beyond the body.

As you ascend up the rungs of the chakra ladder, you may experience intense and renewed energy at any one of the chakras. If this occurs, stay at that level for a while and attune yourself to the energy before going to the next chakra.

Chakra Opening

o Starting at the first level, focus on the center of the chakra, which occupies the same space as the base of the spine. Direct the White Light into this space.

o Now circle the chakra three times. As you pass from band to band, you will be circling farther in an outward direction from the center of the chakra. Visualize the White Energy filling out and charging each band, and as you do so, say slowly: "One, Two, Three."

o Note the direction that you most naturally take when opening each chakra. Do you tend to travel clockwise or counter-clockwise around the chakra? Whichever direction you choose, reverse this direction at the end of your meditation, during the closing phase.

o Upon opening the first chakra, return to the spine and circle upwards around the spine to the next chakra level, about two inches higher. Enter the core of the chakra, and repeat the charging and expansion process into the three concentric bands. Again, say slowly, "One, Two, Three."

o Proceed to the third chakra. Let your intuition guide you as to where exactly this level lies within your body-mind. You will find it between your naval and the solar plexus, just beneath your ribs.

o If you need help grounding, you will probably sense this chakra further down, near or beneath your naval. Visualize the Light flowing into the chakra's core and then in a circular motion through the three concentric bands of the chakra, again, repeat, "One, Two, Three."

o The first few times that you practice, open the lower three chakras as we have done here, and then close them down again. For the precise closing process, see the next section.

o The next time you perform this exercise, provided you feel steady and ready to move forward, proceed to the forth chakra, the *heart center*. Meditate here for a while on the qualities of the Light, then return to the third chakra, meditate here for a while, and close down again.

o Next, move up to the fifth chakra. Meditate here a while, go down to the forth, meditate here a while, then back down to the third, meditate here for a while, and then close back down all the way.

o Next in the sequence, open two more chakras, *both* the sixth and the seventh this time. Meditate a while at the top of your head at the seventh chakra. Then close the seventh and meditate for a while on the sixth. Now close everything down to the first chakra, and finally make sure to close this chakra as well.

o Once you can go up to the seventh chakra easily without feeling out of balance with your lower chakras in any way, you are ready to ascend to the Level of the Rose.

Closing Down

To descend, the opening process described above is reversed. Great attention must be paid to properly closing each chakra, to re-tightening the auric bands, to building a shield of protection and especially to grounding oneself in the body. In this section, the closing down phase is presented as an exercise.

For the complete closing process, see the *Full Rose Way Meditation*, Phase 9, on pages 97-99. For those interested, my book *The Lord's Prayer, The Seven Chakras, The Twelve Life Paths,* can be an enriching adjunct to the closing down phase.

Chakra Closing and Grounding

When closing the chakras, descend from chakra to chakra, entering the largest of the concentric bands first and then circling inwards three times. As you close into the core of each chakra, its bands will return to their normal size, though if you have done everything correctly, each chakra should now be more charged, toned, and vibrant than before you began the meditation.

When we practice returning from the Level of the Rose and the higher levels, you will want to use a more thorough closing process than the initial exercise described in the next section. You can find this on page 60 in Chapter Seven. For now, I recommend that you practice the following closing exercise thoroughly, and that you study the detailed closing process on page 97 in Chapter Nine before commencing the full *Rose Way* meditation.

Please note that while these sequences may look lengthy and you might fear that they are difficult to recall, they really are not. With practice, they will soon come easily and become second nature.

Chakra Closing

o From the highest chakra that you have opened up during the opening exercise, circle inwards sequentially through the three bands, beginning at the outermost band. Circle in the direction that is the opposite of the direction you used to open the chakras.

o When you reach the core of a chakra, pause briefly, and then proceed in a tighter circular motion down around the spine to the next chakra.

o When you arrive, again spiral inwards, starting from the outermost concentric band. "One, Two, Three"— with "Three" at the innermost band.

o Continue down the line, closing each chakra in the same manner.

o Once you have closed the lowest chakra at the base of the spine, continue even further down, with the light in a circular motion, all the way to the soles of your feet. Feel them firmly contacting the floor. Lock yourself into the energy field of Mother Earth to keep yourself grounded.

o Squeeze your hands into fists, then stretch them and gently shake them to release any collected energy. Clench your toes and press your feet into the floor. Then relax.

o Now, imagine that you are wearing a transparent motorcycle helmet that caps the energy around your head.

o Wrap yourself with the luminous silk cloth in the way described in the charging exercise on page 32. Please take a few moments to review that passage. Inhale deeply and exhale as though sighing a sigh of great relief, relaxing deeply into your body.

o Open your eyes and be sure that you have a firm "footing" within your body before you stand.

o Tensing and relaxing your muscles, shutting your eyes tight and opening them, pursing and relaxing your mouth, and patting down your body with your hands are different ways to increase the grounding effect.

CHAPTER FIVE –

The Level of the Rose

The Rose as a Symbol and Experience of Self

In Michael Newton's book, *Memories of the Afterlife*, a woman's spiritual guide presents her with a rosebud that is opening into a beautiful flower[ii]. She feels supported and encouraged by this image, for she understands what the flower represents: her own gradual unfolding into a fully realized soul.

> *"I'm opening up bit by bit, beginning to understand, beginning to show my beauty like a ripening flower. I am on that journey, beginning to understand and to glimpse what the flower could look like—what I could be."*

The eighth chakra, above the crown chakra and mid-way between the body and the spiritual realms, is described by Lu Sen as our own "Spiritual Rose" and as a symbol for the unfolding of our deepest spiritual self. In Dr. Newton's *Memories of the Afterlife*, we learn that a common "first stop" for the soul after death is a beautiful rose garden, where the soul rests and is replenished. In the *Rose Way* meditation, the *Rose* is also our "first stop" where we rest and receive an initial energetic restoration before ascending higher to the White Level. As Joe would say, we are being "recharged" with God's Energy, cleansed and nourished by colors that are held within the White Light.

The *Rose* itself can appear to the mind's eye in different ways, and each nuance has its own meaning and charge. For instance, the *Rose* may have one or more colors, it may be large or small, be a bud or closed blossom, be unfolding, or completely open, fully blossomed. And all of this can change from meditation to meditation, and also within one meditation session, with the *Rose* appearing differently each time.

You might find it natural to imagine yourself sitting inside the *Rose*, or you may be inclined to set aside your body-image altogether and observe the *Rose* from a distance, acknowledging it as a symbol of your developing soul. You might see the *Rose* floating within a dark space, or within a space filled with light, colors, clouds, or other imagery.

You could sense God's Energy and Light surrounding the *Rose*, or feel God's Love as droplets of rain—full of nourishing energies—falling on the petals of the *Rose*. If you are burned out, if you are sleep deprived or locked into a negative thought pattern such as depression, you might see the *Rose* as wilted. If you are going through a deep transitional change, or a cleansing of highly toxic states, even a death and rebirth situation, the rose may be blackish.

Do not be concerned if the Rose is closed, wilted or dark. The Rose will always be restored in the course of meditation.

Remember, whatever "happens" to the *Rose* is actually happening to *you*: *you* are opening, *you* are being nourished and restored, and *you* are entering a higher state of consciousness through your meditative work with the *Rose*.

Ascending to the Level of the Rose

Joe used the image of a white spiral staircase extending upwards from the top of the head as a specific visualization to ascend to the *Spiritual Rose*. While the representation of the staircase is just a suggestion, and you might discover other images that suit you better, try to hold on to the general notion of *circular or spiral motion* as you ascend and descend from the levels.

Through the ascending visualization, you actually are sending a capsule of your own consciousness into the higher levels. As you become more secure in the ascension experience, you can simply extend your awareness upwards in a circular motion to these higher levels.

The distances between the levels can and will increase as your aura evolves. In the beginning, you might sense intuitively that there are only one or two inches between the levels. As your aura is *"charged and recharged,"* as Joe would say, through repeated meditations, the levels may well become denser, thicker, and may be sensed farther and farther apart from one another. The *Rose* may then be felt to be about 18 - 24 inches above your head.

When meditating at the Level of the *Rose*, please note what you see and sense and record it in your meditation journal. Colors, sounds and even smells all contribute to the healing that is being transferred to you.

You may not see your guides yet, but know that they are present, welcoming you into the higher realms, and helping you with adjustments in your chakras and aura.

At this point in the meditation, fine energies are spiraling down into the physical body and the aura, where they have tremendous opening and nourishing effects. In some cases, healing will become evident. I have frequently been able to stop a cold or flu, when symptoms had already become entrenched, by ascending to higher levels and invoking God's healing energy. I'll provide suggestions and explanations for healing with these energies at the end of Chapter Eight.

Joe always invoked God's White Light of Protection while meditating at the *Rose*. According to Joe, without the protection of God's Light, the open *Rose* attracts astral entities. He explained this using a sweet metaphor, "When the flower is open, the bees will come for honey."

To reach the *Rose,* we ascend two complete spirals, from level seven at the top of the head, to level nine, which Joe called the "Level of the *Rose*." To avoid confusion, please note that there is a distinction between the levels at each winding of the "spiral staircase" and the levels of the chakras. The *Rose* resides on level nine, two levels or windings above the crown of the head. The level of the *Rose* is also the level of the eighth chakra.

Ascending to the Rose

o Proceed through the opening steps of the meditation as previously explained, charging the room and your body with God's Energy. Follow up by opening the chakra platforms horizontally, until you have reached the 7th chakra at the crown of your head.

o Now visualize a white, spiral stairway extending upwards from the 7th chakra. Use your imagination to visualize an extension of your spine to act as a scaffold for this stairway. Sense that the staircase's architecture is pronounced and comfortably accessible. Imagine looking up the spiral stairway and seeing a warm, white light radiating down upon you from a sunny level high above you.

o At this point, you can ask that your Spiritual Guide come to pick you up and accompany you to the *Rose*. Do not be afraid to use your mental faculty to synthesize images. Your guides are far from imaginary, and have been waiting for you to establish contact with them.

o You may sense your guide as a presence, as a colored light, cloud, or as a figure. Trust the image that presents itself to you. Know, as you go through the following steps, that your guide is at your side.

o Now, with a keen desire to reach this inviting higher level of sunlight and warmth, see yourself ascending two levels up the staircase, past level 8 and on to level 9.

o As you reach level 9, sense that you have entered a serene location, restful like a beautiful garden. Take a moment or two to perceive the dimensions of this space, and to become used to the higher frequency.

o Now, visualize your *Rose* in this space.

o Ask for God's White Light of Protection, and see your *Rose* surrounded with God's White Energy. Attune yourself to the six qualities of the Light: Peace, Love, Harmony, Balance, Self-Control, and Human Understanding.

o Feel as though you are becoming one with your vision of the *Rose*. Assimilate any impressions that come to you, as you allow this beautiful process to unfold.

o Now, while residing within the *Rose*, feel that your *Rose* is breathing, inhaling and exhaling, in perfect synchrony with your own breath.

o You will intuitively know when you are ready to descend. At this point, extend gratitude to your spiritual guides for their assistance and the healing energies they have so generously shared with you. Then, turning to God, ask God to bring peace and understanding to the hearts and minds of people everywhere.

o Finally, imagine the *Rose* gradually closing from a blossom to a bud. Visualize yourself descending two levels to the 7th chakra at the crown of your head. If you would like, you can see yourself sliding down the stem of the *Rose*, alongside the staircase.

o Imagine that your *Rosebud* follows you and rests in the center of your 7th chakra. Meditate here for a while before continuing with the closing procedure that is detailed below on page 60.

CHAPTER SIX -

The Levels of Heaven, the Evolution of Souls

Joe's Descriptions of the Four Higher Levels

Joe taught that there are four main energy levels above the level of the *Rose*. They have four colors: *white, gold, silver and lavender,* in that order—from lowest to highest. Joe explained that these energy levels correspond to advances in soul development, and are actual realms or dimensions in which spirit life takes place. Younger souls "live" on the lower levels, and rarely ascend to higher levels, "where the master teachers walk." Older and more developed souls can and do descend to lower levels, where they interact with lesser-developed souls.

While these dimensions are outside the physical universe of time and space, souls frequently pass between them. This occurs most dramatically during physical birth and death, but this is not the only way. We can enter these dimensions when we access the higher frequency sheaths of our aura. We do this when we are in deep, dreamless sleep, when we are in a state of deep meditation, and also when we access the "superconscious mind[iii]" in deep hypnosis.

Of the four realms, the lowest, or the White Level, is where the *Rose Way* practitioner will spend most of their time. Here, we meet with our guides and receive energy balancing, recharging, healing, insights, instructions, inspiration, and intuitions. Here, we travel to different spiritual venues and environments—temples, schools, landscapes, starscapes and planets, mountains, forests, lakesides, oceans, gardens, and crystal caves. In these places we can receive spiritual exercises from our guides, and hone our psychic skills. For instance, because we are now within a realm that is outside of time, we might receive visions of both the past and the future. Because we are outside of space, we can experience what is known as "remote viewing."

However, what we see and what we can achieve here is determined by our level of spiritual development, and by ethical and karmic concerns. I talk more about psychic experience in the context of the Rose Way *meditation in Chapter Eight.*

Ascending to the Higher Levels

During each of Joe's classes, he would lead us first to the *Rose* and then to the White Level. Here, we would meditate quietly for about half an hour. Still in this ascended state, we then would open our eyes and practice psychic exercises with each other in small groups.

Occasionally, Joe led his classes up beyond the White Level to the Golden Level. Less frequently, he would lead us up still higher to the Silver and the Lavender Levels.

It is difficult to put in words what it felt like to ascend all together to these levels in a group of twenty or more persons. Group meditation has a certain magnifying and containing power. In Joe's class, I always felt balanced, held, and protected when on the higher levels—whether White, Gold, Silver, or Lavender. I always felt grounded and well connected to my body after closing down—perhaps because we all descended and were grounded together.

Over the years, I have gone up to the Gold, Silver and Lavender Levels on my own several times. I only recommend this practice for someone who is thoroughly experienced and spiritually advanced—and very well grounded.

Please understand that neither I nor anyone who knows the *Rose Way* believe it to be a dangerous process. However, there is a risk that if practiced prematurely on one's own, grounding back into one's body from these higher levels could be problematic. For instance, you might feel tired and "spaced out" several days afterwards, until your aura has again completely contracted into your energy system.

It is critical to make sure that you close the chakras, ground out, and perform all the other cautionary measures as directed. Do not try to have experiences that are beyond your level of development—do not take any short cuts—to assure only highly beneficial experiences.

Directions to the Levels

The four higher levels referred to here can be understood as extensions of the higher sheaths of the aura, called the "cosmic body" in some metaphysical systems.

- Level of the Rose – 9, two winds up from the 7th chakra
- White Level – at level 11, two winds above the *Rose*
- Gold Level – at level 22, eleven winds higher
- Silver Level – at level 33, eleven winds higher
- Lavender Level – at level 44, eleven winds higher

Michael Newton's Descriptions of Soul Levels

Dr. Newton describes four main levels of soul evolution, from lowest to highest: white, gold, blue, and purple. Newton's statements are founded on the corroborating accounts of thousands of persons in deep hypnosis. Like Joe, Dr. Newton reports that souls at different stages of development "live" on their respective levels in heaven, and that whereas higher souls can journey down to teach younger, less developed souls, the latter do not travel up to the higher levels.

Joe's Four Levels = White, Gold, Silver, Lavender

Newton's Levels of Souls = White, Gold, Blue, Purple

I find it interesting to compare Newton's four soul stages and Joe's four energy levels, and I am confident that they are interconnected. In the introduction to his book on hypnosis techniques, Newton encourages innovative approaches. He writes, "I recognize this material may also be useful for those who wish to employ alternative methods to reach the spirit world;" and, "The application of different approaches to the mind can only enhance our knowledge and perspective of our spiritual life."

The *Rose Way* is just such an alternative method and "different approach," and Newton's detailed work will give the seeker wonderful insights into ways that the *Rose Way* can be adapted to help individuals on their spiritual journeys. I'd like therefore to take a moment to briefly summarize Dr. Newton's work, especially his revelations of heavenly journeys and the development of souls.

Dr. Newton has learned from his patients, while trans-induced to a superconscious state, that each and every one of the countless souls created by Source is unique and contributes a precious and wonderful gift to the totality of creation. As they accumulate experience, talents, thoughtfulness, and wisdom, souls change their energetic quality, or color. The main colors that distinguish soul development are *white, gold, blue,* and *purple*, with other colors present in the aura reflecting special talents and character traits.

The foundation for soul evolution is free choice and free will. We are allowed to make mistakes so that we can see the consequences of our choices. Through countless reincarnations, which are carefully planned together with our guides and our soul group, we become adept in the use of emotional, mental, creative and ethical skills. After death, we return to the spirit realms where our energies are cleared, healed and restored, and where we can process the lessons of our lifetimes.

Here, souls of the same level of development reside in groups of "soul friends" on the same frequency level. In the same way that parents guide their children, more highly developed souls visit the younger souls, supporting their education and development as beloved teachers, guides, and helpers.

In stark contrast to our life on earth, there is no judgment in these realms regarding "older or younger," "wiser or more naïve," and certainly no judgment as to "better or worse." All souls are genuinely motivated to grow more cognizant of the nature of reality, and each strives to develop and to practice their unique gifts. Each soul knows itself to be of equal value in the grander scheme of things.

Here, I think of my favorite Bible quote, John 4:19, "We love Him because He loved us first." On earth, we may sometimes struggle to maintain an appreciation for the value of life, but in heaven, we experience that the very fabric of reality is held together by the Love and Light of God, and we respond by being naturally energized and determined to evolve toward that Light.

Yes, all souls naturally respond to the Creative Force by wanting to grow closer to it. Like children of a beloved parent or elder, souls have a heartfelt wish to "pitch in" and help with the process of creation and the maintenance of an orderly and loving universe.

In Appendix One, I include a list of books and website that I recommend you follow up on. They will surely compliment your work with the *Rose Way* meditation.

The "White Level"

If you have practiced the preparatory exercises and if you feel steady in your meditation practice, you can now ascend to the White Level. Please resist any temptation to jump ahead, or to practice ahead. There is a precise and meaningful sequence to learning the *Rose Way* meditation.

To Ascend to the White Level

o Meditating at the Level of the *Rose*, visualize the white staircase again, and ascend two more windings.

o If you would like, you can ask your guides to pick you up at the *Rose* and accompany you to the White Level.

Meditation on the White Level

Energetically, the White Level will feel completely different from your usual emotional and mental states. Should you have wondered what it feels like to be immersed in higher frequencies, now you will know! It's much like a rapid change in altitude, like taking off in a jet, or ascending from deep water back to the surface.

Take some time to get accustomed to the new sensations. There is no race, no hurry! Schedule about thirty minutes to dwell here. You might find yourself slipping down back into your *Rose*, or back to the top of your head. If this happens, do not be concerned. Simply visualize the white spiral staircase, and ascend again. If you have not yet done so, it will be helpful to ask for help from your spiritual guides, and to allow their presence to enter your conscious awareness.

People will have quite different experiences on the White Level, even the first few times that they ascend. It depends greatly on personal soul development, on previous experience with meditation, and on our ability to be in attunement and in contact with our guides and the environment on this level.

Joe would therefore *not* prescribe one specific form of silent meditation. It was understood that some of us would spend time interacting with our guides, while others would engage in quiet, abstract meditation—focusing, for instance, on the pure positive state of God's Light that is characteristic of the White Level.

Inviting your Guides

Each of us has one main guide and sometimes one or more secondary guides. Because our guides live in metaphysical space, they are never "far" from us, though they can be far from our awareness and consciousness. When we ask sincerely that our guides come to us, our invocation reaches them immediately. Because they exist in a dimension that is outside of time, they are instantly here with us.

We might then have a sense of *knowing* that our guides are near, or we might sense an increase of light, peace, or other color or quality. When we feel their presence, we might also see or sense their faces or figures, vaguely or in detail. But it is also entirely possible that we will not perceive any visuals at all. In this case you simply need to *trust* that they are with us.

Your guides will help you adjust to being open and expanded at the Level of the *Rose* and at the White Level. They will see and be fully aware of the energy exchanges that are flowing between the great Universal Source and your aura, chakras and energy systems. I will talk more about your interactions with your guides in Chapter Eight, and how the symbols, objects and messages that they give you can help with your healing, growth and transformation.

CHAPTER SEVEN –

Exercise to Completely Close the Chakras

Because the *Rose Way* meditation powerfully charges the psychic centers and expands the aura, it is important that the practitioner close down properly. This is a bit analogous to the importance of closing down a computer system in an orderly way. Sometimes you may have thought you closed it down, but you come back later and see that it stalled in the process, potentially damaging the system or leading to a loss of data. All of this is to emphasize again the importance of the chakra closing process that I explain in detail below. Following these directions, the bands of the chakras will return to their normal width and the energy bodies will be fully anchored in the physical body.

Because closing down is so important, I have presented it three times in this book at various stages of expertise. The first time was on page 43 in Chapter Four, when you practiced descending from the different chakras, and finally from the chakra at the top of the head.

Then, you learned how to descend from the *Rose* on pages 49-50 in Chapter Five.

Here, you will learn how to descend from the White Level. I will include some extra steps at the level of the *Rose* and throughout the closing process that will bring the full benefit of the meditation into your energy system.

At the end of this book in Chapter Nine on pages 97-99, you'll find the closing process described again as the final closing phase of the complete *Rose Way* meditation.

I emphatically recommend that you practice the exercises in the order presented here. You may find it helpful to repeat the closing process multiple times at the conclusion of a meditation session. Only if you are able to clearly feel what it is like to have completely reconnected with your body should you explore the higher levels through the *Rose Way* meditation.

Closing the Chakras

o   Conclude your meditation and approach the staircase on level eleven, the White Level.

o   Here, take leave of your spiritual guides by thanking them, and by acknowledging any messages, objects, or symbols that they may have imparted to you. If you would like, you can you're your eyes and make a note of the messages, symbols, etc., in your meditation journal before descending.

o   Now imagine the spiral staircase, and, either alone or together with your guides, descend two windings to the Level of the *Rose*.

o   Take a moment to revisit your flower. Become absorbed in the image of the *Rose*. If you would like, you can open your eyes and in your journal, note any changes between your *Rose* as it appeared at the beginning of your meditation (color, form) and at the close of your meditation.

o   Ask that dewdrops of White Light fall upon your *Rose*. Feel your *Rose* covered in drops of bliss. Feel the light sparkling on all the petals. Its qualities stream down into your body.

o   Consciously feel the six qualities of the Light in every cell of your body: Peace, Love, Harmony, Balance, Self-Control and Understanding.

o Now pray that peace and human understanding be extended to all the people of the world, especially those who are suffering, hungry, and oppressed, and that they be strengthened by God's love, peace, and harmony.

o Finally, pray for those you love, for those in your prayer circle, and so on. You may also pray for yourself.

o Now, it is time to close the chakras. Descend two windings, down to the top of the head.

o Imagine the *Rose* above you now, closing slowly, brimming with radiant light, peace, and bliss.

o On the top of your head, see the three expanded bands of the seventh chakra. Starting at the outermost band, circle inwards three times to the center of the chakra, "Three, Two, One." As the energy of the chakra returns to its center, feel that the *Rosebud* is pulled down into it from above. Now the *Rosebud* is contained within the closed seventh chakra.

o Now spiral down to the next level, where the bridge of your nose meets your forehead, in the center of your skull. Again, imagine the three bands of the sixth chakra, and starting at the outermost band, spiral inwards to the absolute center, "Three, Two, One." As you visualize the sixth chakra close, draw the *Rosebud* down from the seventh chakra into the sixth.

o We are taking the higher energies down from chakra to chakra. Continue to close each chakra in the same way... Spiral down to the throat chakra, "Three, Two, One." Do not hurry.

o Between each chakra, give yourself time to visualize the Light spiraling down around the spine to the next chakra. Each time, close the chakra by traversing the concentric bands to its center. Draw the Rosebud from the chakra above into the center of the chakra you are closing.

o   Close each chakra, moving from the heart chakra, to the solar plexus chakra, to the chakra at the base of the abdomen, and then the chakra at the base of the spine.

o   Here again close your chakra, and draw the *Rosebud* down from the chakra above it into the first chakra's absolute center.

o   Feel your energy extending down into your feet, and through the floor and into the earth below. Then cap the energy above your head with your crystal helmet, and drape yourself in a floating, translucent white fabric that comes together, as if tied, beneath your feet.

o   Now, open the *Rosebud* that is at the base of your spine. Imagine it opening into a small flower. Feel its energy radiate up from the flower throughout your body and out into your aura. Feel the qualities of the Light. Stay with this Light for a moment. Then close the *Rosebud* again.

o   You can open and shut your *Rosebud* at the base of your spine as needed over the next few days. Whenever you do, breathe deeply a few times to integrate the Light and its uplifting qualities again into your system. Always remember to close it again. Your *Rosebud* will eventually need "re-charging" in the spiritual Light of your next meditation.

Note: As previously mentioned, if you wish, you can top off the shutdown process by taking a few moments to feel the connection of your core energy through your feet to the earth. If you are having problems feeling this connection, you could stand in bare feet on the grass in your yard, on a stone or concrete patio outside, or in the basement. You could also stand in a damp bathtub or shower stall, allowing water to run over your feet, or let water run over your hands at a sink, to neutralize any excess charge that might remain and to take you more fully into your body-connection and awareness.

Spacing the Full Meditation

It is up to you to decide how often to practice the full *Rose Way* meditation. This decision will vary with your unique needs, and can range from several times a week to once a month—or even once a year. You must discern for yourself how the meditation helps or hinders you in your present "pattern" as Joe would say.

Ask yourself, "How much time do I need to re-connect with my physical body when the meditation has concluded?"

"How much time do I need to process what I have experienced while on the higher levels?"

"How is the full meditation serving me? Is it enhancing my other spiritual and healing practices?"

"Is it helping me refine my psychic tools?"

"Am I able to integrate it into my professional and personal life?"

"If I am a student, is it helping me to concentrate on my studies?"

"If I am an artist, is it helping me delve more deeply into my art?"

"Or is it taking me too far out of my body, making me feel spaced-out and separate from others?"

"How is it affecting my interpersonal relationships with my family, neighbors, and fellow workers?"

As with all spiritual tools, we are encouraged to use them, but not to misuse or abuse them. When we use them selfishly, or foolishly, it does come back on us according to laws of karma.

Once you are well established in your spiritual discipline, ask yourself as well, "How is my practice affecting me so *that I can be of service to others?*"

Many great souls throughout history have held that service is the highest of all spiritual practices. Are you bringing the Light into your school or workplace? Are you standing up for your truth, while also being more in harmony with your family, friends and colleagues?

Use the *Rose Way* wisely, being sure to stay grounded before and after, and it will remain a great resource and become ever more useful, effective, and helpful to you and the world around you.

CHAPTER EIGHT -

Practicing the Higher Senses

Teachers of psychic practices encourage their students to give "readings" in order to activate and understand their psychic senses. Joe developed his own system called "Chaldean Numerology and Astrology" for this purpose. This system may one day be taught again, but for now I suggest that you study one of the many accessible arts, such as astrology or the tarot. My personal favorite is the ancient Chinese system of the "I Ching."

I have found that having the "tools of the trade" physically in my hands activates a deeper connection to the intuitive processes. Rather than practicing online, use a deck of real tarot cards, learn how to cast your own horoscopes, and refer to physical books when you consult the I Ching.

Laws for Communication with the "Other Side"

Most of us are not born psychics. We do not see deceased people and other disincarnate entities from childhood on, nor do we automatically experience remote viewing, knowledge of future events, or telepathy etc. If we try to consciously develop our psychic abilities, it is most often because we hope to attain an increased appreciation for the spiritual dimensions of ourselves as human beings. And, of course, for many of us, it is to become more useful to Spirit as healers and bearers of the Light.

As far as communicating "through the veil," or with guides on the "other side," it is helpful, at the very outset, to understand that the transfer of information follows an ancient and hallowed code of ethics that is in place to protect us, and to keep us straight on our path. These laws are explained in many resources for psychic development. I was happy to discover them also elucidated in the books of Dr. Michael Newton, who received this information directly from the higher selves of his patients in deep hypnosis.

As Newton explains, life is a kind of school in which we practice skills, take or re-take tests, teach others, and learn new lessons. In order for the earthly classroom to be effective, we agree, while still in the spiritual world, that as part of our life's contract we will experience a kind of amnesia toward both our former existences and toward the lessons we have committed to learn this time around. Only by being fully in the dark can we test our mettle as a soul and engage in the lessons to be learned. The "tests," the "dramas," and the "struggles" that we have set up so carefully, often in conjunction with others, would not work very well if we retained full knowledge that we are eternal beings and that what we are seeing with our earthly eyes is essentially a form of illusion. Only when the veil is tightly drawn can our life's challenges impart the lessons they were designed to teach.

It is therefore not ours to know all things.

In fact, there may be entire areas of knowledge that our soul consciously blocks out in order to concentrate on the specific lessons that we have come to learn this time around. It turns out that our guides, too, are constrained in what they can tell us, and also in how much they can help us. In truth, they are not allowed to exert much influence when it comes to almost all of our major lessons in life. Even our guides have to follow a strict code of ethical conduct. As Newton points out, "Sometimes it's not in the soul's best interest to have easy answers[iv]." The first law around communication with guides therefore is this:

1. Our guides will not tell us how to live our life.

They may in select cases, alert us to challenges, give us healing colors and symbols to help us become more whole and vital, and they may give us hints about people and events in our life. *But the responsibility for our choices is always ours alone.* Only by exercising free will, and by taking responsibility for our choices and their consequences, can we truly grow.

Why? Free will is a sacrosanct element of our existence. It is only when we learn to freely choose the right way, the right thing to do, that we develop real "tested" virtue. As Newton writes,

> *"Both guides and elders are in the business of stimulating the gradual development of a soul's ability to improve on their decisions toward making better choices in each new life[v]."*

The second rule follows naturally from the first:

2. We are only given information that we are ready to receive and that is ours to know.

What this means for the practitioner of the *Rose Way* is that even after ascending to the spiritual *Rose* and the White Level, and even after getting into contact with our guides, we might not receive the information that we *want*.

The reverse law also holds. According to the code:

3. We will not get the information that we want if we are not ready or if it is not ours to know.

Take this into consideration when you address questions toward your guide(s). You probably shouldn't ask whether you should marry John or Larry, Melissa or Sue, or ask if you should live in the city or country, or if you should invest in stocks or bonds.

If you do ask these questions and repeat them, even though you sense that no true answer is forthcoming, your guides will probably laugh and play with you until you understand that these kinds of questions are not appropriate to your relationship with them, in most cases.

If, however, you do receive information from your guides that purports to tell you how to live your life, suspect 1) that you might be imagining the message, 2) that your spiritual guide is feeling mischievous, 3) that this is one of the rare times when you actually are receiving concrete direction (the exception that proves the rule).

About Guides

Each of us has one main guide. There is a feeling of great love and familiarity with this guide, whom we have known since we were very young souls. We *know* that this entity has our very best interests at heart.

We may have other guides as well, but one central guide is our main teacher. The love that passes between the two of you is ineffable and infinite. He or she may even have incarnated with you and may have been a parent, spouse, child, or mentor to you, possibly in multiple visits to this home we call Earth.

This primary guide, however, is not usually a fully enlightened being, but is still evolving, learning, and involved in various projects—one of which is supporting you as you go through your challenges.

Our guides will help us according to agreements we have made with them before birth. For instance, we may have "contracted" that we will feel alone and separate during parts of our life, for the sake of our personal growth. To this end, we may have asked our guides to promise not to help us at certain points.

Learning to be truly compassionate is the single most important purpose of life on this plane, where we have bodies and minds that can feel pain, experience loss and deprivation, and know fear. Through such earthly suffering, souls gain depth and above all learn empathy and compassion.

We may also have agreed that we will go through exceptionally good times when we feel supported by our guides and by the universe, and when we know that we are never truly alone. Through feeling such connection, our soul is affirmed in its essence and purpose.

Our guides do connect with us within the *Rose Way* meditation, and regardless of what we might sense, see, or hear, we can be sure that our guides are participating in energy adjustments to our aura and chakras. This helps us be filled with positive, uplifting energies, so that we can move through our life's lessons with more confidence.

Interacting with our Guides

When you first meet your guide, he or she—your guide might also appear as an androgynous, genderless being—may appear as a vague figure or face, or as a clear image. It is just as possible that rather than seeing your guide, you will *feel* your guide, as a presence or focus of light or energy. At this point, ask if you may know your guide's name. You might hear only an approximation of your guide's spirit name—they can be difficult for us humans to hear and pronounce. Trust what your imagination tells you.

There are several ways that our guides can involve us in adjustments to our energy systems. When we note the color of a guide's robe, for example, we become aware of an energy color and quality that is *being directed toward us*. If we receive a gift, such as a mineral or gemstone—which once again may be perceived through the faculty of imagination—this, too, will represent the quality of energy that is being channeled toward you and with which they want you to be involved.

Sometimes, *Rose Way* practitioners will see images or symbols. Dr. Michael Newton writes that the symbols we are shown by our guides represent our talents and accomplishments from past life times, and are meant to give us confidence in face of our present challenges. Whether we understand these symbols or not, they will affect our subconscious minds and move us toward greater understanding.

Once again your trusted meditation journal is useful at this point: make notes about your interactions with your guides. Note the name(s), any colors you see, and any message, object or symbol that your guide presents to you. In the days following such a meeting, try to incorporate the colors you were shown into your life, and contemplate the objects or symbols you may have received.

If you receive a gemstone or metal from your guide, read about its properties and meditate on its image in the following days. Should you possess an actual piece of the metal or gemstone, clear it energetically and hold it in your hands during meditation, or keep it in your pocket or beneath your pillow. Your guide may be using this particular kind of metal or gemstone to affect changes in your aura.

The same holds true if you are shown a plant, flower, medicinal substance or treatment, book, painting, landscape, or other object that holds special meaning for you. Hold these images close to your heart, and if you can find the actual plant, book, or landscape, spend time with it if possible over the next several days. Think about the meaning of these objects, these places, these pieces of knowledge, and strive to discern what your guides are trying to tell you. Such colors, symbols, or objects might also appear in your dreams. Write about these processes and discoveries in your meditation journal.

Rest and Restoration

Each of us has hopefully had some special experiences in life when a place or scene inspired profound feelings of peace, awe, depth, and connectedness. You may have already noted some of these special places in your meditation notebook when you recorded key experiences that can help you attune to the six qualities of the Light. As you meditate on the White Level, ask your guides to take you back to one of them.

If you are uncertain about which place or scene is best for you, ask your guides to remind you of the most appropriate place, and to take you back there now, while you are meditating. You can also ask your guides, "Please take me to my special place of peace and renewal on the White Level," and then be open to "see" which special place is revealed to you. Keep the superb faculty of your *imagination* active and trust the images that present themselves to you.

When I go up to the White Level, I often find myself being taken to a place where I am told that I am receiving restoration. I sense gentle and wonderful energetic charging, and am grateful to return again and again to these inner temples and gardens for more energy and healing, which enable me to establish clearer steps as I navigate through my life.

Dr. Newton and other experts on the subject have noted that after physical death, souls often visit a garden or nature setting, to rest and renew their energies before moving on. This rest often includes a cleansing shower of healing energy. Joe, too, invoked a blissful fall of "rain-light" before closing the *Rose*; its energy seemed to descend upon the petals of the *Rose* with the most gentle and restorative of powers. I encourage you to invite experiences of gentle rain, drizzle, or dewfall, and to see yourself sitting by a stream, brook or body of water during your White Level visualizations.

A small temple or crystal cave might be another restorative setting. While sitting in this inner place, you may become aware of a vibration or buzzing, or of a soft, penetrating light that cleanses your body-mind. In one of my recent meditations, I found myself standing in a crystal cave, placing my hands on the crystal walls. It was a powerful clearing experience.

Here are some examples of other scenes that you might see:
o Open, blue, light-flooded skies
o Mist-covered meadows
o Open views over mountains
o Lake scenes
o Ocean scenes
o Night skies, dotted with stars
o Deep space

As your practice goes on, you may be pleasantly surprised to find that more and more beautiful memories will gently become "unearthed" and naturally return to your recollection. Make note of them when they appear. Your list will lengthen.

Dr. Newton's books, as well as those by many others who have researched near death and between life experiences (see

Appendix), can also be studied to gather ideas about landscapes and schools and other activities that reside on the White Level and the levels above it. You may find yourself going to some unusual places with your guides, and Dr. Newton's books, so rich in detail, may very well serve invaluable reference points to help you more fully understand your experiences. But you may well find that your very own memories and insights are the most vivid and powerful of all in helping you with your spiritual practice.

Communication with Your Guides

After a period of rest and restoration, you might want to try to converse with your inner guides. Communication with your guides and other similar psychic experiences are not necessary elements of the *Rose Way* meditation. Think of them as optional and sometimes desirable adjuncts, for even if you cannot hear or sense your guides, you will nonetheless benefit from their presence and their healing.

The first several times that I went up to the White Level, a chorus of jubilant singing received me with the words, "Rejoice! Rejoice!" I felt as though a throng of angels was celebrating and inviting me to join in their festivities.

It was actually quite a while before I came into conscious contact with my guides—such as seeing them within a beautiful garden scene, hearing their names, and being informed about ways to call on them for help. Even then, I hardly received anything akin to a personal message. I was very young, and was not ready to receive hints about what life had in store for me—I wasn't ready to process higher spiritual teachings or guidance.

I do believe, three decades later, that even after I had learned how to "hear" the words of my guides, I initially received messages mainly because I dearly *wanted* contact—as affirmation of spiritual realities—and not because I *needed* to hear their messages.

It takes a leap of faith to begin writing down words as they come into your mind. Do not be afraid to use your *imagination*, the part of the mind that can synthesize images and also auditory stimulation or hearing. It serves as a window through the veil.

At first, receiving and writing words from the "other side" may feel like free association, like a free flow of dissociated words and images. This is absolutely fine! Consider it progress that you have taken the initiative to try in the first place. You might find that you sense words distinctly at times, and other times, vaguely. The sentences might wander. You might have a hard time keeping up with them. You might think that your meditation is triggering your own wisdom, and that you are hearing your own insightful thoughts, nothing more. Accept, in the beginning, that you are probably receiving a mixture of your own words and thoughts and those of your guides. *Don't worry*. Overcome your natural hesitations, and continue to *write* what you sense being projected to you, or what you feel moved to write.

Remember, too, that we only receive what we are ready to receive and what is ours to know.

As you advance and make progress, you may find that at times the words come through in a coherent manner, while at other times they may be jumbled again. Stretch your awareness toward what you sense as the edge of your consciousness, and then relax in a receptive attitude. Wait and listen. It takes practice to become a fluid "translator" of the energy that is being focused upon your consciousness by your guides.

With practice, I eventually learned to sense the "otherness" of the messengers that were working with me. As I continued to practice, I felt more clearly that the words and messages I received were projected onto my mind, rather than coming from within my mind; that I was catching them, funneling them in, rather than producing them from the inside-out.

Occasionally, I received a large download of information. One time, I scribbled pages and pages with notes that were basically a map of how my life would unfold, the important persons and teachers I would meet, and the lessons I had to learn in the following few years. If you receive such a "download," simply go with the flow. Using your meditation journal, record the messages as best as you can and trust the process.

Receiving Messages in Daily Life

Now and then your guides will connect with you in daily life. Once you have received messages from your guides while in meditation, it becomes easier, in the course of everyday life, to notice when the unusual thought or voice in your mind carries a certain quality—a beautiful sense of lightness, joy and resonance—that does not seem to be fully your own.

When this happens to me, I often do a double-take and ask myself if it was my own thought, or if I may have received a communication from my guides. If the latter, I will usually become aware of a certain *knowing* in my gut.

Just a reminder here, as we are discussing messages that we receive in daily life—professional psychics aim to close off their psychic centers when going about their daily activities. You should not consciously try to be receptive to psychic messages and activity during everyday life, as it can be exhausting.

Again, a reminder of what we have already discussed—regardless of what you "hear," the choice or decision as to how to respond to the message is always your own. Just because you receive a tip from your guide does not mean that you have to take it. It is through *free will* that we learn and evolve, and sometimes a tip or suggestion is simply our guide's way of pointing us to an opportunity to exercise free choice, regardless of whether, in the end, we decide yes or no. Your guide may be giving you a nudge to direct and *test* your decision-making processes—and not to give you the answers for what you should do.

You might also sometimes receive a telepathic message from someone who is thinking of you strongly. In my own experience, these messages feel different from messages that come from my guides. Telepathic messages feel more as if they are inside my own nervous system, as though beneath my skin, a feeling or sense in my body, while a message from my guides feels more like a small, angelic voice in my head, resonating in my sixth and seventh chakras.

In my case, my guides used to frequently announce when I was about to meet someone important. In my "wild twenties" I met quite a few very unusual people "by chance." These meetings obviously required a lot of organization on the part of my guides, and they were announced enthusiastically on the day before or the morning of the meeting.

One time, I was writing letters while sitting in a café, and a voice came into my mind insisting that I get up "right now!" so that I could run to the bus stop. The urgency was so striking and persistent that I actually found myself running a mile in heels along a wet, sloppy autumn road, wondering if I was crazy. On that same bus, I met a Dutch professor of history who was visiting the area. He became my lifelong friend, and opened my mind to areas of study that later were central to my artistic and intellectual development.

The messages and teachings we receive daily life are deeply personal, and often have to do with our own challenges. When I lived in a busy city, I frequently heard the question, "Do you love them?" referring to the masses of people walking along the streets. "God loves everyone," I was reminded. And that reminder is right. Love is the way.

When we begin to develop ourselves spiritually and psychically, especially with the *Rose Way,* which is infused with love, we are called upon to recognize each other as children of God and to love each other. In fact, the more we develop our powers, the more we are expected to exercise love, not only in our actions, but in our deepest thoughts about others, as well.

Remote Viewing

When the psychic centers are open and we actively project a part of our mind to a place or person, we in a sense "go there" and "see" the matter we are thinking about. This practice, popularly known as "remote viewing," presumes that a part of our consciousness is able to access the entire universe—independent of time and space.

"Think it, and you are there," is a phrase commonly used by practitioners of this skill.

The levels of Heaven are beyond time and space. It is impossible for humans in our normal state of mind to conceptualize this existence, yet the psychic apprentice works with the assumption that our inner senses do in fact have access to such dimensions.

Remote viewing is not really difficult. Generally, focusing on persons and places that are familiar can suffice to bring in some degree of information. This is actually fairly normal for mothers—for instance, we might send a mental probe to our children when they are away at school, register that everything is as it should be, and go on with our day.

With the practice of the *Rose Way* meditation, certain remote viewing abilities may develop, and even without conscious intention, you might find yourself playing with them in everyday life, and keeping your psychic muscles active. For instance, I often imagine a clock if I want to know what time it is. If I really "look," I can often see the exact time. Similarly, if I have to wake up at an unusual time in the morning, I will set the alarm clock, but I will also set my inner clock five minutes earlier, to wake up in time to prevent the noisy ring. This has worked well for me and for many others who have tried using similar approaches—in fact this is fairly common among people with a psychic leaning.

In Europe, where many people travel every day by bus or trolley, I often found myself waiting for my commute. For fun, I would sometimes send my mental probe along the route of the bus until I sensed that I had found it. Then I traveled mentally with the bus through the city, stopping at its stops, "watching" people enter and leave the bus, until, finally, I watched as the bus turned onto my block just at the moment when my mental image indicated that it should. I was right on the mark enough of the time that it was fun to do. And with this exercise, I used otherwise empty "down time," putting it to good use rather than being bored or impatient.

I liked to also apply remote viewing when studying history—concentrating on a place and a time and letting my mind "go there" to pick up on whatever it might sense. This made the study much less dry and impersonal.

One time, when I was traveling abroad and I was thinking of my boyfriend, I went up to the White Level and wrote a list of questions to him in my journal. Then, still on the White Level, I concentrated on him and asked respectfully to speak with him on the soul level. I then wrote down what I thought were his soul's answers, and I had a vision of sitting down, writing as well.

Remarkably, several days later, I received a letter from him in which he had written down and answered all the questions I'd asked, and it was dated from the night of my meditation.

Respectful Viewing

Practitioners of the *Rose Way* are expected to be especially respectful of the abilities this meditation may impart. While remote viewing can be intriguing, and fun, and many games and experiments can be designed to explore this ability, remote viewing—especially when it has been activated by or is in any way associated with the sacred nature of the *Rose Way* meditation—must be treated with great respect.

Remote viewing can tread dangerously close to a breach of privacy. Good psychics emphasize that we should always respect others' privacy and never peek inside the thoughts or the life of another individual unless specifically asked to do so by that person.

Anyone involved in remote viewing is also well advised not to draw any major conclusions or make any major decisions based on what they have seen during remote viewing, for the process is not infallible. When conducting business, for example, it is obviously better to rely on standard face-to-face conversations.

Respecting others' privacy is a universal law on the higher levels. According to Michael Newton, relationships between souls in our afterlife existence are, in no small part, guided by a mutual respect of privacy. In our heavenly home, where telepathy and transparency make each of us an open book, we simply do not look into parts of others' stories that are not freely revealed to us.

I suddenly had to laugh while writing this. I just remembered that when I was in my early twenties, I had an unexpected experience involving remote viewing. I had recently separated from an important boyfriend. Although living apart, we were still committed and were trying to resolve our problems. One night, while meditating on the White Level, I happened to think of him. One thought, a single glimpse with remote viewing sufficed. Instantly I saw him—having relations with someone else. I saw her figure, the color and length of her hair—even other details. Later we became friends, and she confirmed the date of their first relations.

As things turned out, it was very helpful for me to have this information. I did not know it yet, but this man would continue to sabotage his relationships for decades to come. The information I received through remote viewing, though painful at the time, allowed me to quickly disentangle myself from the relationship. I was thus able to move on and save myself untold pain and heartache. I must have been meant to receive this information. The fact that I had received it while practicing the *Rose Way* was reassuring to me— my guides had given me this glimpse.

As you advance in your psychic development, you may find that your guides show you certain kinds of information through remote viewing. Any person whose psychic abilities are refined enough to practice remote viewing, and whose guides instruct them in its proper usage, will also intuitively be aware of the right ways to use this skill.

When you do get a remote read on someone, never forget that you are doing so with the help of your guides and that you are only allowed to remote view if the following conditions are met:

It is yours to know.

You are ready to receive it.

You are able to handle the information respectfully and responsibly.

The main point to keep in mind here is to be immaculately ethical and avoid viewing others who have not asked to be viewed, in the very same way you would avoid peeking into another person's open window at night. Most likely, this would hold karmic consequences that you would not wish to accrue. And again, always remember that the *Rose Way* is a sacred meditation and that the abilities or "powers" which flow from it must be treated with great respect and humility.

Getting Visuals—A Reminder

When I began attending Joe's classes, I noticed that some of the students had an easier time getting visuals. They described their travels, meetings and experiences on the White Level in great detail. For my part, I struggled pretty much with all the visuals such as the Spiritual Rose, inner landscapes, my guides, and so on. When I tried to *see* my Spiritual Rose it seemed to me that I was creating an "imaginary" rose instead. When I turned to my guides, I saw only a blur.

The most important step for me, as I learned to work with visuals, was allowing myself to accept whatever came to me, rather than second-guessing the process. I had to gradually learn to believe in myself and in the variances and the range of what I was seeing and sensing.

This may be the case with you, also, as you progress along your path. Don't expect to always see or perceive with the same clarity. You, too, will come to know the range of your visuals. As they will probably change and develop with time, I suggest that you record them in your meditation journal for future review and reference.

Receiving a Personalized Meditation Form

When I started out on the *Rose Way,* thirty-five years ago, it was not easy to find information about meditation. I realized at the time that the *Rose Way* meditation was not a traditional form of meditation with established practices. I began to yearn for more and different meditative exercises to teach me some of the basics such as calm focus in stillness, scanning the body, and so on—practices that today you can easily learn in basic meditation courses. With no other recourse, I asked my guides to show me exercises to help advance my meditation practice. I wrote down what I heard, and began to practice with much success. One exercise was a landscape: I was supposed to focus on a certain aspect of it, to practice leveling and balancing my focus in stillness. The other exercise had to do with sensorial perceptions.

If you are desirous of new exercises, consider asking your guides for meditation practices that are best suited to you, and try those recommendations. Of course, we only receive specific guidance from our guides *if we are ready, and if it is ours to know*. It is well worth a try, however, to ask.

Contact with the Deceased

Personally, I have known only one person who was born with the ability to see the souls of the deceased, and who sees them every day in her waking consciousness. This ability is very rare. The three exceptional psychics in the New Zealand television series "Sensing Murder" (available on YouTube) all report having seen deceased persons since childhood.

I have only seen the souls of recently deceased persons three times: my beloved Grandmother, my husband's Great-Aunt, and a neighbor who died of drug overdose. In all three cases, I did not know about the death at the time that I received the distinct visions and visits.

I was blessed to be able to be present at my mother's death, to be alone with my father's body soon after he died, and also to attend my mother-in-law's three-day wake. There is a very special and sacred atmosphere around death and the deceased, and I encourage seekers to be open to the lessons of love that the passing of our family and loved ones brings to us.

Michael Newton writes that the souls of the deceased may stay around for a while to comfort those they left behind. I felt this keenly when sitting with my father's body after his passing. I could feel his presence as clearly as if he had still been alive—perhaps even more closely and intimately.

Although I did not hear specific words spoken to me, I could receive his love and his intentions and meaning. Sitting with him for a few hours, I could share many things that I hadn't been able to say to him during his life, because he had been an atheist. It was a blessing for me, and brought about a much better sense of closure.

Birth Announcements

At the beginning of each of my four pregnancies, I received a joyous announcement from the child's guide, sharing pertinent information with me. I found that both early pregnancy and the days after birth were special times when I was extremely receptive to messages from the children's guides, and also to visions of the child's upcoming life.

Our dreams while pregnant may also provide fascinating clues about the soul that is incarnating through us. Keeping a dream and meditation journal during pregnancy is a good idea. In the decades to come, you may derive comfort and guidance from these insights, and be amazed by how telling they may prove to be.

Past Lives

When I began studying the *Rose Way*, I was extremely curious about my past lives. One night at Joe's class, after asking my guides humbly for a past life vision, I saw myself as a young, run-away slave, living about 2,000 years ago in northern Africa. The vision was brief, but terribly clear. I saw myself resting on the slope of a sandy hill, out of breath in the morning sun, exhausted, frightened, looking off to a town on the horizon, and thinking about the punishment I would incur if I were caught.

The vision left me shaken. Of all things to see—a vision of fear and suffering was not at all one I had expected. Thinking it over, though, I realized that my adolescence carried an emotional quality of trauma that was similar to the vision.

Perhaps I had not only been a slave in prior life times, but had also treated other people as if they were slaves or pawns? Perhaps most of us have had lifetimes on both sides of the oppressor-oppressed spectrum. And perhaps having had my own heavy dose of this experience again in my life had served to help me appreciate the importance of freedom and respect for all human souls.

In that first year with Joe, I sometimes caught a glimpse of myself as a Native American, camping by a tranquil lake. It was gloriously quiet there in the twilight beneath the trees, a kind of silence that is so hard to find today. I believe that my guides were saying, "Remember this peace? Remember this harmony? It is your special place you can always return to. Now, work for it today."

Over the years, I've received many other insights into past lives while in meditation or on the edge of sleep, a state called "hypnagogia." Through dream interpretation, I've come to understand how the lives I have experienced might still be influencing me.

I have not often gone to psychics, but I am happy to say that the two times I did go, I encountered persons of real integrity who used their roles ethically. Unfortunately, friends of mine have been hurt by their interactions with psychics who posed as advanced spiritual teachers and told them what to do.

One time, a dear friend acted as a psychic for me. I was twenty when I taught her the *Rose Way* meditation. She was a skilled and accurate tarot reader and could instantly access greater psychic abilities through the meditation. On the White Level, I shared with her the names of a few important people in my life, including my father and three past boyfriends. She received detailed visuals immediately, including symbols and several scenes from lives I'd shared with each of them.

The reading helped me understand why these relationships had been so intense and also in part destructive. In the years that followed, I brought each of these relationships to a higher level of mutual respect and understanding.

Today, I do not actively seek information about my past lives. I know that if it is mine to know, the information will come to me. Occasionally, I do receive a past life vision or insight that ties into the present in some way. I appreciate these insights, as they help me understand why I feel drawn to certain kinds of work or projects, and they do enrich my sense of purpose and life.

Seeing the Future

A few times in my early twenties, I went up to the White Level and did a practice that my guides showed me. We called it "looking down the road of life."

It was simple. I would imagine myself looking down a road and walk upon it. The landscape the road passed through represented the atmosphere or "pattern," as Joe would say, around the next several months. Landmarks, such as rivers, buildings, tunnels, portals, intersections, animals, people, or flashes of color, represented events that I was likely to meet up with and pass through.

As I walked down the road in my vision, I would write my impressions and get a sense of a timeline. I usually saw about four months ahead. And at the end of that period, I could review how the major events I'd seen on the road did correspond to events that had occurred in my life.

As I've mentioned, I did most such future meditations in my early twenties. This is a time when so much is still open about one's life, and that open quality, with so many choices ahead, can be confusing and conflicting.

As well as road mapping, I occasionally received personal information in the form of a flood of messages that I would write down and treasure.

Today, I have a strong sense that I am not supposed to look ahead, and so I do not.

Meeting our Demons

Today, many spiritual researchers believe that there are no such things as demons, devils, or dark spirits. When we encounter visions of such entities in meditation or in hypnosis, we are simply meeting parts of our own personality that have been disassociated or disowned by us in the past, possibly due to events in childhood and adolescence.

The encounter with such disowned parts of ourselves is closely linked to Carl Jung's concept of "shadow sides," and many therapists offer so-called "shadow work" to help us recognize and reintegrate these parts back into ourselves.

In her book, *Eastern Body, Western Mind*, Anodea Judith, Ph.D., applies Jungian psychology to address the shadow sides that are associated with each chakra, offering a solid basis for re-integration through chakra healing.

As to my own opinion, I do in fact believe there may be astral entities who are not very evolved. They are not evil, however, or demons, but because they are not evolved they may be drawn emotional energies that are familiar to them. The point to note here is that when we re-integrate our shadows, these entities are no longer drawn to us.

Therefore, if you do encounter dark feelings such as fear, guilt, shame, rage, hatred, etc., in your dreams and in meditation, recognize them as signals from your subconscious mind. They are your own soul's cry for healing and wholeness and not the influence of "demons."

Healing

I describe here three simple but powerful energy applications that are based upon the *Rose Way* invocation and the circular channeling of God's Healing Light.

Responding to a Cold or Flu

If you are coming down with a cold or flu, you can practice the *Rose Way* to either halt the progression of the illness or to minimize its effects.

For instance, you may feel yourself coming down with something while at work or school. When you finally arrive at home, go to bed, but sit up in bed and do the exercise that follows below.

Then lie down, cozy and warm beneath the blankets, and rest for as long as possible—overnight, preferably.

Other healing support is also recommended if available: Echinacea (five capsules at the onset of a flu or cold), a cup of boiled water to warm yourself, and other favorite home remedies.

White Light Clearing

To begin the exercise, first ascend to the level of the *Rose*, and then to the White Level.

Here, pray for God's White Healing Energy.

Feel it enter your body through the top of your head and visualize the Light filling your body. It flows in a circular motion, spiraling down into your hands and feet.

Often, flooding the body this way with God's healing energy, especially from the open state of the White Level, will stop a cold or flu right in its track.

Remember to close down completely and ground yourself.

Stopping a Sore Throat:
Focusing God's Healing Energy through Your Hands

If you are experiencing an infection that has already taken hold, it will often manifest first as a painfully raw or sore throat. In this case, cup your hands close to your neck, just beneath your jawbone, so that you cover the front of your chin in the lower parts of your palms. If you are sitting, you can find this position by placing your elbows on the table, pressing the base of your hands together, and supporting your head in your palms, with your fingertips just behind and below your ears.

Your hands naturally have an energy field that concentrates within the chakras located in the palms. If you are experiencing a sore throat, these chakras are now encasing the area at the back of the mouth, which typically becomes sore at the onset of infection.

While simply cupping the energy fields in your hands over your throat can help beat off infection, it is much more powerful if you involve the White Healing Energy of God by using techniques of the *Rose Way*.

Envision energy entering your body through your head as follows:

o Cup your hands over your throat, as described above.

o Invite the White Energy into your space, and see yourself surrounded by White Light.

o Ask that the Healing Light of God now enter the top of your head in a circular motion.

o See it spiraling down through your head, and into your neck.

o At this stage, envision the light penetrating your entire throat, including the area that is painful. Dwell on that area. Penetrate and saturate it well.

o Now see how the Light circles down through your shoulders into your arms and down to your hands. See how the Light flows out of your hands into the chakras of your hands, and then flows into your throat where it surrounds and penetrates the area that is painful.

o You will immediately notice that when the Light reaches through your hands and into your throat, there is a much more powerful and palpable energy flow than before you applied the *Rose Way* visualization technique. Continue to surround and penetrate your sore throat with God's Healing Energy.

o Repeat the visualization occasionally, to renew the flow of energy from the top of your head into your hands and throat.

I have used this healing modality numerous times and have found that it can reliably fight off an infection. If I am able to respond right away, it may only require twenty minutes of application while in a sitting position. If the infection is more advanced, it may require keeping my hands on my throat during sleep, and periodically waking up to mentally repeat the visualization and renew the energy flow.

Circling Energy for Multiple Healing Applications

The circular energy flow that we practice with the *Rose Way* can act as a source of healing throughout your life.

Any time that an area of the body becomes painful or inflamed, mentally invite God's Energy through the top of your head, and send a circular flow of energy to the area.

Tiny vortices of energy will loosen muscles and tendons, and work in all the joints to release tension and reduce pain.

You can mentally send tiny circular currents of energy to any part of the body, to all the organs, to the nerves, to your eyes and ears, and to muscles that are tight and knotty.

Finally, during daily life, by working with the image of tiny flurries of spiraling vortices of White Light, flowing in a downwards direction from above the head into the feet, and into the chakras a few inches beneath our feet, we improve our experience of focus and of being grounded.

CHAPTER NINE –

The Full *Rose Way* Meditation

Phase 1 - Invocation

Close your eyes and breathe deeply in and out, three times.

Shake your hands three times to release stagnant energy.

The invocation (please feel free to adapt this invocation as best befits your beliefs and understandings):

"In the name of the Father, the Son, the Holy Spirit, and – (say your own name) – ask now that God's White Energy come to you in a circular motion and that it fill the room from the floor to the ceiling, and that God's Light impart to you its qualities of Peace, Love, Harmony, Balance, Self-Control, and Human Understanding."

Phase 2 - Charging

Now say "May God's White Energy enter my body through the crown of my head."

Visualize the white energy concentrated above your head, and then sense the Light circling down your head.

The Light continues to fill your body, always moving in a circular motion, down through your head and neck to your shoulders, down the arms, into your hands.

Shake the hands three times to complete the flow of energy through the fingers and to release any negative energy.

The Light returns up the arms to the shoulders, then down your torso and spine to the hips.

As you scan your body, you may become aware of tension, energy blocks, or pent up areas within your physical body or around your body in the aura. Ask that the Light release these conditions, breathe deeply, and imagine the darkness dispersing as the area fills with light.

From your hips, circle with the Light down to your feet, then out through your feet into the ground.

Pause, and sense balls of energy beneath the soles of your feet, and then travel with the Light back into your feet, up your legs to your hips.

Here at the base of the spine, you will find yourself at the level of the first chakra, and ready to begin the opening of your chakras.

Phase 3 – Chakra Opening

Go into the center of the first chakra at the base of the spine with the White Light.

Circle the chakra three times, charging each band of the chakra: "One, Two, Three."

Feel the qualities of the Light: Peace, Love, Harmony, Balance, Self-Control, and Human Understanding.

With the Light, return to the spine and circle upwards around the spine to the next chakra level. Circle the second chakra three times: "One, Two, Three."

With the Light, return to the spine and circle upwards around the spine to the next chakra level, at the solar plexus. Circle the third chakra three times: "One, Two, Three."

With the Light, return to the spine and circle upwards around the spine to the next chakra level, at the heart. Circle the chakra three times: "One, Two, Three."

With the Light, return to the spine and circle upwards around the spine to the next chakra level at the base of the neck. Circle the chakra three times: "One, Two, Three."

With the Light, return to the spine and circle upwards around the spine to the next chakra level behind the forehead. Circle the chakra three times: "One, Two, Three."

With the Light, circle upwards to the next chakra level at the top of the head. Circle the chakra three times: "One, Two, Three."

Feel the qualities of the White Light all throughout your body: Peace, Love, Harmony, Balance, Self-control and Human Understanding.

Phase 4 – Ascending to the Level of the Rose

Visualize a white, spiral staircase extending upwards from the top of your head. Imagine looking up and seeing a warm, white light radiating down upon you from above.

At this point, you can ask that your spiritual guide come to pick you up and accompany you to the *Rose*. You may sense your guide as a presence or as a color of light, or as a figure. In any case, know that your guide is with you.

Ascend the winding staircase two flights: past level 8 to level 9.

As you reach level 9, sense that you have entered a serene location and visualize your *Rose* in this space.

Here, ask for God's *White Light of Protection* and imagine your

Rose surrounded with God's White Energy. Attune yourself to its qualities: Peace, Love, Harmony, Balance, Self-Control and Human Understanding.

Behold the color or colors of your *Rose* and any other impressions that come to you.

As you become one with your vision of the *Rose*, see yourself surrounded by the Protective Light.

Feel that your *Rose* is inhaling and exhaling along with your own breath, soaking in the gentle Light.

Phase 5 – Ascending to the White Level

From the Level of the *Rose*, visualize the white staircase and ascend two more windings to the White Level. If you would like, you can ask your guides to pick you up at the *Rose* and accompany you.

Phase 6 – Individual Meditation

You have arrived at your personal portal to eternity. Here, begin your individual meditation.

Phase 7 – Psychic Exercises

After a period of restorative personal meditation, you may interact with your guides and engage in exercises for your psychic development. Before descending, you may open your eyes at any time and make a note of your experiences in your meditation journal.

Phase 8 – Descending to the Rose

Conclude your stay on the upper levels by returning to your personal portal on the White Level.

Here, take leave of your spiritual guides by thanking them, and by receiving any messages, objects, or symbols that they may wish now to give you. Make a note of the messages, symbols, etc., in your meditation journal.

Before descending, you may wish to attune yourself again to the qualities of the Light.

Now imagine the spiral staircase, and descend two windings to the Level of the *Rose*.

Sit within the *Rose* and come into attunement with it. In your journal, note any changes between your *Rose* as it was at the beginning of your meditation (color, form) and here at the close of your meditation.

Ask that dewdrops of White Light fall upon your *Rose*. Feel your *Rose* covered in dewdrops of bliss. Now, ask that dewdrops of golden light fall on your *Rose*. Now, of silver light. Now, of lavender light. Feel the drops of Light sparkling on all the petals, their quality of bliss streaming down into your body.

Feel the qualities of the Light in every cell of your body.

Now pray that peace and human understanding be extended to all the people of the world, especially those who are suffering, hungry, and oppressed, and that they be strengthened by God's love, peace, and harmony. Pray for those you love, for those in your prayer circle, and so on. You may also pray for yourself.

Phase 9 – Chakra Closing

It is time to close the chakras.

Descend two windings, to the top of your head, and imagine your *Rose* now above you, slowly closing, filled with radiant light, peace, and bliss.

At the top of your head, imagine the three expanded bands of the seventh chakra. Starting at the outermost band, circle inwards three times to the exact center of the chakra, "Three, Two, One." As the energy of the chakra returns to its center, feel that the *Rosebud* is pulled down into it from above. Now, the *Rosebud* is contained within the closed seventh chakra.

Now, spiral down with the Light to the sixth chakra, on the level of your forehead.

Imagine the three expanded bands of this chakra. Starting at the outermost band, spiral inwards to the absolute center, "Three, Two, One." As you visualize the sixth chakra closing, draw the *Rosebud* down from the seventh chakra into the center of this chakra.

You are taking the higher energies down from chakra to chakra.

Take a moment to attune yourself to the qualities of the Light: Peace, Love, Harmony, Balance, Self-Control and Human Understanding.

As you continue to close, give yourself time to visualize the Light spiraling down along the spine from chakra to chakra.

Now, spiral down with the Light to the fifth chakra level, your throat chakra.

Imagine the three expanded bands of this chakra, and starting at the outermost band, spiral inwards to the absolute center,

"Three, Two, One." As you visualize the fifth chakra closing, draw the *Rosebud* down into its center.

Now, spiral down with the Light to the next chakra level, at the level of your heart.

Imagine the three expanded bands of this chakra, and starting at the outermost band, spiral inwards to the absolute center that is aligned with the spine, "Three, Two, One." As you visualize the forth chakra closing, draw the *Rosebud* down into its center.

Spiral down with the Light to the next chakra level, the solar plexus chakra, which lies beneath your ribs.

Imagine the three expanded bands of this chakra, and starting at the outermost band, spiral inwards to the absolute center that is aligned with the spine, "Three, Two, One." As you visualize the third chakra closing, draw the *Rosebud* down into its center.

Spiral down with the Light to the next chakra level, which lies in the lower abdomen.

Imagine the three expanded bands of this chakra, and starting at the outermost band, spiral inwards to the absolute center that is aligned with the spine, "Three, Two, One." As you visualize the second chakra closing, draw the *Rosebud* down into its center.

Spiral down with the Light to the next chakra level, which lies at the base of the spine.

Imagine the three expanded bands of this chakra, and starting at the outermost band, spiral inwards to the absolute center that is aligned with the spine, "Three, Two, One." As you visualize the first chakra closing, draw the *Rosebud* down into the absolute center at the base of the spine.

Feel your energy extending down into your feet and through the floor, into the earth below. Then cap the energy above your head with your crystal helmet, and drape yourself in a floating, translucent white fabric that comes together, as if tied, beneath your feet.

Now, imagine the *Rosebud* at the base of your spine opening into a small flower. Feel its gentle energy radiate throughout your body and out into your aura. Feel the qualities of the Light. Stay with the Light. Thank God for the gift of this Light. Then close the *Rosebud* again.

You can open and shut this bud at the base of your spine as needed over the next few days, to remind yourself of the profound spiritual energy you have been allowed to assimilate into your energy system. It will eventually need "re-charging" in the spiritual Light of your next meditation.

Breathe three times again slowly, and open your eyes.

Thank you.

CHAPTER TEN –

Who Was Joe Koperski?

If you delve deeply into the *Rose Way* and experience what it has to offer, you may develop a natural curiosity about the man who brought it to us in modern times. The following six sections are presented for those who want to know more about this unique teacher and how he brought the *Rose Way* into this world for us to use and enjoy.

My own clearest memories of Joe are that he was even-tempered, articulate, concise, friendly but never familiar, and rarely if ever sick (I know this because he never cancelled class). In my mind's eye I see him standing at the chalkboard—smiling, joking gently while explaining a new concept in "Chaldean Astrology"—a tall man with very fair skin, a bit baggy beneath the eyes, always looking well-washed and wearing short sleeved, crisply ironed plain cotton shirts. Over the years that I knew him, his dark sleek hair would thin on top and grow longer in back.

I close my eyes and see Joe walking around the classroom, speaking quietly as he coached us in small groups. When he wasn't teaching, he was generally sparse with words, reserved, polite. If he spoke to you personally, it was taken to mean something. There was very little small talk with Joe.

The last time I saw Joe Koperski was summer of 1981. Five years had passed since I'd left the Los Angeles area and I was back only briefly, visiting my mother.

I found him in the yellow pages. He had moved to a nice little house in the hills of Chatsworth. The new classroom was smaller, his students, older. When I walked through the door, he smiled and seemed pleased to see me—though in his usual way, he didn't make much of it.

There was so much I wanted to tell him—about my psychic development, how I had taught the *Rose Way* in Germany and Switzerland, and that I had developed a set of exercises with the *Rose Way* that taught and developed energy sensitivity. But I didn't say any of these things. It suddenly didn't seem very important. Instead, I listened to Joe's gentle, warm voice while he led us in meditation, impressed yet again by his unswerving devotion to teaching, and poignantly aware that this was the last time we would meet in this lifetime.

An Interview with David St. Clair

As you can tell from the paragraphs above, I am not able to tell you much about Joe Koperski. I was still a child when I knew him, and it did not occur to me to ask him personal questions such as where he was born, what he had done before teaching meditation, or if he had been married. Fortunately, a journalist named David St. Clair did ask Joe these questions when he interviewed him for his book, "The Psychic World of California[vi]," published in 1972. I'll summarize their interview here. Whenever I use Joe's own words from the book I'll frame them with quotation marks.

St. Clair introduces us to Joe, whom he calls the "Sage of Topanga Canyon," by saying he comes highly recommended and is a well-known medium in Los Angeles.

Joe seems happy to share his story with the journalist. He says that he was born in Toledo, Ohio, and that he had his first psychic experience in his twenties. While asleep in bed with his wife, his foster mother had appeared to him, and, touching his hands, had woken him to say good-bye—she died soon after.

Joe says that he served in WWII before coming to Los Angeles to work as a technician in the television industry. At that time, other psychics in Los Angeles pointed out his spiritual potential to him, and he felt motivated to work in the occult and to serve humanity with his talents.

However, when he tried to devote his life to helping others through spiritual work, he encountered serious problems. The first time, his motives were wrong: he wanted to attract fame and money, and so he says he "was stopped." The second time, he was too emotionally involved, and he again had to stop. The third time, he was doing well, channeling several entities as a medium, and he had a large following. However, he grew uncomfortable being "a puppet" for the entities that came through him, and he stopped of his own accord—this time, he thought, for good.

Then, on Easter Sunday, 1968, Joe was approached by his master teacher, Lu Sen, who proposed that they work together. (According to Michael Newton's revelations about the spiritual world and its hierarchies, master teachers are more highly developed than one's personal guides.) Lu Sen fused his consciousness together with Joe's, and now Joe could communicate with Lu Sen whenever he wished, without going into trance. Later, other advanced teachers also fused with him and Lu Sen, and all were now available if he called on them. "They are taking me into a pattern of knowledge that is almost like the beginning of time," Joe tells St. Clair, "like back in Atlantis."

Lu Sen's teachings were called "Chaldean Astrology and Numerology," and "The Chaldean *Rose Way* Meditation."

Chaldea is an older name for the Mesopotamian region, which includes Babylon, Sumer, Akkad, and Assyria. This region is the earliest known origin of western civilization, and is also the source of the earliest known records of astrology.

Joe tells St. Clair that Lu Sen has shown him a new way to view the human aura, with 21 distinct auric bands, and three main horizontal bands around each chakra—positive, negative, and neutral. While today, this three dimensional view of the aura does not sound revolutionary, at the time, 1968, it was quite new.

Joe also tells St. Clair that our problems today are often related to unresolved problems from past lives. By going into a higher vibratory plane and looking at a person's aura, Joe could read everything about their past life conflicts. He would then "take a person back" by "making the trip" himself, and energetically release those conditions that hold a person in a negative pattern today.

When Joe began working with Lu Sen, they attracted a large following. Joe taught four classes a week, with 20-30 students attending each class. I'll describe his classes in detail later.

Joe tells St. Clair that everyone has psychic abilities, and that they are stronger or weaker depending upon our experiences before and during birth. He says that we can't know the extent of our gifts until we practice and explore them. He explains however that while his classes are designed to help people explore their psychic gifts, their primary purpose was to teach how to tune in to God's Light, and to use this ability to aid and assist others—however our individual paths might unfold.

Joe tells St. Clair that after death, we return to higher realms where we attend school. When our lessons are processed, we may choose to return to earth or to another realm or planet to continue our development.

In reply, St. Clair asks Joe if anyone can ever possibly lead a pure enough life that we can say it is our last, to which Joe says, emphatically, "I *know* this is my last lifetime."

St. Clair describes Joe as a large, gentle, soft-spoken man in his late forties. He describes Joe's house on Topanga Canyon Blvd as "rather battered, filled with charts, incense, candles, folding chairs and books."

To me, Joe's house seemed as if it had been converted from a storage or business space into a classroom. Any bedrooms or kitchen would have been incidental and small.

However, I have to say, learning to meditate and discovering my inner, sacred place of stillness, even while heavy traffic roared by just outside, was truly a tremendous experience: spirituality does not depend on pretty decoration or a serene environment. It resides in one's own being, one's core.

St. Clair tells us that any of Joe's 200 students could attest that multiple spirit entities came through him when he was in trance. This is odd because I personally never saw Joe go into trance or speak in a voice that was not his own. In fact, Joe was emphatic that we should not go into mediumistic trance when practicing the *Rose Way* meditation, but that we should always maintain possession of our own consciousness. Perhaps St. Clair was referring to a previous phase of Joe's work as a medium.

Through research into public documents, I have learned that Joe was born 1923, that he moved to California in 1951, that he was married once, but did not have children. Joe died in 1993 in Chatsworth, California. Now, in 2013, two decades later, I am deeply moved to honor his life and his work with this book.

Three Personal Teachings

As I mention above, Joe was sparse with words. If he ever did say something that seemed even a tad personal, you felt that you should listen.

Three times, Joe said things to me that went beyond the lessons he was teaching in class.

One Saturday morning class, I had persuaded one of my best friends to attend with me. Joe drew me aside and said, "This one is a keeper, a life-long friend." He looked at me meaningfully.

I was confused. Of course she was a keeper! She lived across the street from me and, for five long years, had been one of my dearest and closest buddies.

However, in the years that followed, a series of events did lead to the loss of our friendship. Perhaps Joe had been giving me a warning.

Another time, he said, meaningfully, "Your aura has black flecks in it. Your faith is not complete."

I had no idea what this meant. But years later, I realized that one of my life's greater challenges is to let go of controlling patterns, and to live more fully and completely aligned with my knowledge of the Light.

The third lesson was less direct. I had arrived at his house early one evening and was surprised to hear angry voices through the closed front door. Entering, I found Joe standing across from two young men. The atmosphere was sizzling.

Now Joe said to them, "You come to my home and demand that I acknowledge you! You say that you are special! I should acknowledge that you are special! Do you see that girl there?" He pointed to me. "She was my daughter in a past life! But I give her no special treatment. Because she's not special! And you're not special! *I'm* not special. *We're all special!* Do you understand?"

The men got his point, and the atmosphere lightened. Later, Joe said no more to me about their exchange or about our past life relationship. That was that.

For my part, I have to admit that I found reassurance in the thought that our teacher-student relationship might be part of a long-term soul contract. We had known each other before. There was a reason that I came so often to his class.

Yet, all of us have our deeper connections and long-term development plans. It's not unique! We're all special!

Evening Classes

Joe gave classes four times a week. On Monday, Wednesday and Friday evenings, from 7:30 to 10:00 or 11:00 pm, he taught the *Rose Way* Meditation in combination with psychic development. Saturday mornings he focused on astrology.

A straw basket for donations was set next to some candles and incense for sale on a table in the entrance. You gave what you could afford—and this enabled me, very poor at the time, to participate. On another table lay booklets on meditation and astrology that he had authored, printed out and stapled together. They contained the rudimentary basics of his teachings, and cost five dollars each. I still have my copies.

To begin, Joe led us through the chakra opening part of the *Rose Way* Meditation. This phase could last twenty minutes or longer.

Personal meditation time was allotted about a half hour. For each of us, meditation was different. For most, it involved meeting with guides and traveling to landscapes, classrooms or cities. It might include a vision or insight, such as receiving a message or symbol, or perceiving with clear awareness one's energetic changes.

After personal meditation, we did not immediately close down the chakras. Instead, we would spend about an hour of sharing, learning and practicing different exercises while remaining up on the "White Level."

To begin, Joe turned on the lights and invited us to share what we had experienced in meditation. Then he went on to explain the new material that he was channeling from Lu Sen, before asking us to work alone or in groups of twos or threes. As we practiced, he'd walk around the room and stop at each group to see how we were doing.

The last part of class was devoted to closing the chakras and drawing the bands of the aura close around the body. This phase was just as important as the opening phase, and lasted about as long.

Before we closed completely, Joe would say a prayer for the rest of the world, full of vibrant compassion and energy. I always felt embraced by a profound and sacred space when Joe led this prayer.

Saturday Morning Classes

On Saturday mornings, from 9:30 to 12:00, class focused on what Joe called "Chaldean Astrology and Numerology," a system that he was receiving from Lu Sen.

In these classes, Joe would lead us briefly in the *Rose Way* meditation so that we could study in an energetically open state. A few times, Joe taught new components to the *Rose Way* meditation during Saturday morning classes, and when I realized that new meditation forms were coming through on Saturday mornings as well as in the evening classes, I rarely missed them.

Joe's Energy Healing

Joe gave healings as needed, and one night after class, I had the opportunity to watch him give a hands-on healing up close.

A woman had recently been injured in a car accident. Joe placed his right hand over her mid-back area and told me how he worked, first with emerald green energy, penetrating the injured tissue, and then surrounding the area with a protective band of golden and then lavender light.

Joe occasionally shook his left hand, drawing it away from her body, as though pulling out and eliminating the stagnant energies around the injury.

As I looked on, not knowing what to expect, I saw radiant colors extend around his right hand, radiant green and then brilliant gold.

While in the years since, I have often seen the transparent colors of auras, the color that was projected from Joe's hand that night was so concentrated as to appear solid. I couldn't believe my eyes. To date, this remains the strongest visual of a healing energy that I have ever had. Of course, I was still energetically charged from the *Rose Way* meditation, so my perception was heightened. But I believe that the colors were so brilliant because a brilliant master healer was channeling them.

Closing Words

I have written this book with the sense of it being something I should do—a kind of coming full circle with the teachings that were given to me, and passing them on to a new generation.

My daughter says that I should contribute a few more pieces to this puzzle and publish a *Rose Way* Meditation Journal and a set of energy and psychic exercises that I developed long ago to teach together with the *Rose Way*. I might do that. I also have in mind to publish what I remember about Joe's astrology and numerology system, and a *Rose Way* guidance CD. If you are interested in pursuing what you have read about here, keep your eyes open for future works.

Please give me feedback. Find my email address on my blog, and write me about your experiences with the *Rose Way*. I look forward to hearing from you.

About group meditation: I do recommend ascending to the higher levels (Gold, Silver, and Lavender) in a group situation so that you can experience what this is like. As, in the next few years, experienced meditation teachers begin to offer classes in the *Rose Way* meditation, this group experience may become increasingly available.

With enough interest, I will be offering *Rose Way* Accreditation to teachers who demonstrate their teaching experience and their full comprehension of this method. If you are looking for a teacher, I will list those with *Rose Way* Accreditation on my website (that presently is still in progress): www.rosewaymeditation.com.

Alternatively, Joe Koperski suggested that we practice the *Rose Way* informally in groups of people we trust. Such groups could base their practice on the *Rose Way* guidance CD that will be coming out in 2014.

It is my dear hope that practitioners of many directions will discover this jewel of a meditation and integrate it into their work. A strong, intuitive sense that the *Rose Way* might yet come to new blossoming is really the energy that is motivating this publication. I am entrusting you with a great gift; please develop it as befits your understandings, use its benefits responsibly and only for the higher good, and pass it on again.

Appendix

Recommended Reading

How to Know God:
The Soul's Journey into the Mystery of Mysteries
by Deepak Chopra

The great value of this book is that it provides a map for spiritual development, describing the ways and stages in which this development expresses itself over many lifetimes.

Creation by Gore Vidal

Gore Vidal was a controversial and eloquently outspoken man, as well as a great historian and thinker. Whenever asked which of his books he wished to be read, he answered unequivocally "Creation." It is a down-to-earth, fictionalized exploration of the origins of several eastern religions, told from the point of view of an ancient Greek student of life.

Evolution Angel by Dr. Todd Michael, Ph.D.

In this book, Dr. Todd Michael, a medical doctor, minister, musician and artist, shares the profound spiritual insights that he received through his personal conversations with angelic beings. Dr. Michael entered this intuitive state of communication during life and death situations that he encountered as the director of an emergency ward. His insights encompass universal mysticism and world religions, and explore the very nature of existence.

Journey of Souls, Destiny of Souls and Memories of the Afterlife, by Dr. Michael Newton, Ph.D.

Many people have written about their personal near death experiences. Many psychics and psychic channels (such as Abraham-Hicks, Jane Robert's for Seth) have channeled the insights they have received about the soul's existence through their advanced abilities and their contact to advanced ascended teachers. While these teachings are extraordinary, Michael Newton, a clinical psychologist and hypnotherapist, is the only resource that describes the soul's existence based on prolific evidence and clinical research, rather than on an isolated psychic phenomenon.

Originally an atheist and skeptic, Newton reached his conclusions only after compiling thousands of accounts of the afterlife from patients who were carefully trans-induced into the superconscious state of hypnosis, in which the core soul personality becomes the speaker. Don't miss this amazing resource.

Staying Connected: How to Continue Your Relationships With Those Who Have Died (a collection of lectures from 1905 – 1924) by Rudolf Steiner.

Rudolf Steiner was an Austrian philosopher and spiritual seer. His influence is felt today in the US and around the world in Biodynamic farming and in Waldorf Schools. He reached his conclusions about the afterlife through his own clairvoyant penetration of the spirit realms. Steiner believed that the core experience of Christ is essential for spiritual evolution, and has been criticized for his Christ-centric view. Nevertheless, his insights into the spirit realm are profound. This work is translated from early 20th century German, and some find the language stilted. However, it contains seeds of wisdom and is worth the effort.

The Oversoul Seven Trilogy
by the psychic channel of "Seth," Jane Roberts.

A wonderful, fictionalized account of the ways in which one's many lifetimes and inter-dimensional experiences interact and enrich the education of a developing soul. With these charming books, Roberts condensed the thousands of pages that she channeled from the Seth entity into an enchanting and easy-to-understand read.

Initiation by Elizabeth Haich.

One of the first teachers of yoga in Europe, Haich wrote this book for her advanced students to illustrate how a previous incarnation in the Egyptian priesthood had influenced her spiritual path this lifetime. The stories of her two lifetimes are framed against the pre-war culture of Germany and the initial stages of covert experimentation in psychic phenomenon in Europe. Many people find this book life-changing and inspirational, a dive into the poetry of existence.

Hero or Victim? by Meredith B. Mitchell, Ph.D.

Dr. Mitchell, a certified Jungian psychologist, frequently taught seminars at UCLA in the 1970s. When his students implored him to write a book, he spent many years producing this marvelous collection of his lectures. Unable to find a publisher, he eventually self-published (it is not unusual that publishers turn down good books). Using fairy tales and myths, Meredith illuminates the ways that an understanding of Jungian archetypes and shadows can catapult us into greater consciousness, positive life choices and confidence.

Prayer and the Five Stages of Healing by Ron Roth, Ph.D.

Those who are drawn to my books often come from a Christian background and moving into a larger, mystic and world-religion perspective. Dr. Ron Roth, a Catholic priest for many years, encompasses the same expansive spiritual path in his book, "Prayer and the Five Stages of Healing." This book, which offers a collection of prayers, describes a path of "healing into wholeness" through joy and suffering. It is not written exclusively from the Christian point of view, but it incorporates and addresses that view.

Wheels of Life by Anodea Judith, Ph.D.

This book addresses our energy system and chakras, and is accessible even for beginners. Those who are advanced will find reminders of valuable knowledge and insights. I have listed it here, not because it is far better than other books on the subject, but principally because in Chapter 9, *The Return Journey*, her descriptions of the sensations of moving from the highest to the lowest chakras are valuable to the *Rose Way* practitioner as we learn to close down the chakras after meditation.

I admire all the popular authors on chakras and appreciate all their works. I suggest that you read through the reviews on amazon.com, listen to the author's speak on online videos, read their websites, and intuitively choose one or more books to begin with, if chakra work is something you are interested in pursuing.

The Lord's Prayer, The Seven Chakras, The Twelve Life Paths
by Dana Williams

Please also take note of my own contribution to the subject of chakras and astrology as they align with the great Christian prayer with its immense potential for guidance and healing. The unique chakra meditation described in this book is based upon the *Rose Way* meditation, and is superbly grounding and renewing.

---

[i] Prayer and the Five Stages of Healing, by Ron Roth, page 89
[ii] Memories of the Afterlife, by Michael Newton, page 39
[iii] Terminology from Michael Newton
[iv] Memories of the Afterlife, by Michael Newton, page 61.
[v] Memories of the Afterlife, by Michael Newton, page 55
[vi] St. Clair, David. *The Psychic World of California*. Bantam Books (1973), ASIN: B0006W1IM6

www.ingramcontent.com/pod-product-compliance
Lightning Source LLC
Chambersburg PA
CBHW030119170426
43198CB00009B/673